THE
CLUE
BIRD

THE
CLUE
BIRD

Sage advice for the young and not so young

R. WAYNE BROWNE

TCB Publishing, LLC
Tucson AZ
2025

TCB Publishing, LLC
thecluebird.com
Copyright © 2025 R. Wayne Browne
All rights reserved.

TCB Publishing, LLC | P.O. 65648 | Tucson AZ 85728
www.thecluebird.com

Library of Congress Cataloging-in-Publication Data
Names: R. Wayne Browne
Title: The Clue Bird – Sage Advice for The Young
and Not So Young / R. Wayne Browne.
Description: First Edition. | Arizona: TCB Publishing, LLC, 2024
Identifiers: LCCN 2025913667 (print) | ISBN 978-1-965892-00-8 (hardcover)
| ISBN 978-1-965892-01-5 (paperback) | ISBN 978-1-965892-02-2 (ebook)
LC record available at https://lccn.loc.gov/ 2025913667

Cover & Editing: Kuyomi Books
Illustration: Lenine Karamesha

This is a work of creative nonfiction. Some names and identifying details have been changed to protect the privacy of those mentioned. The conversations in this book all come from the author's experiences and have been retold in a way that evokes the feeling and meaning of the experiences in accordance with the author's recollection.

To my grandchildren

Contents

INTRODUCTION

WAY BACK IN THE eighties, I became a single parent. I had to raise my children alone when they were very young. Unfortunately, I had no father to copy because my dad was a non-returning POW in the Korean War. Although I didn't know how to be a parent or a dad, I vowed to be the best father I could be to my kids. Armed with no experience, I was simply at a loss. However, in that moment, I decided to be the father to my children that I never had.

Faced with the biggest job I'd ever struggle with, having no experience, no personal training, no manuals, no books, or any *how to be a dad* guideline to bolster my performance, I realized I'd probably make mistakes. Doing this and doing that would be just fine with me as long as I gave it my best. It was simply *game on* as they say. My mantra was: you're going to make many mistakes going in. Embracing my situation, I promised myself to always own up to and correct my mistakes on the spot and then move on. What I knew is... I would always be around and available to my kids on a nonstop basis. Doesn't every good dad want that?

From the start, when faced with a dilemma concerning them, I privately looked into a mirror and asked myself a simple question: "What is the best decision I can make at this very moment for that child?" When the answer came, I did just that—no matter what. That made it simple. It was never about the cheapest, easiest, or quickest thing to do. For me, the answer was whatever seemed the best thing to do in that moment as it pertained to my child.

At first, I used my military training and decided to attack the small stuff every day. No days off. No slacking. I always looked for deviations, with a commitment not to allow sliding in our house. Being an efficient dad, I checked rooms for cleanliness and organization, dealt with homework, checked grades, and set new goals when needed. As

I believe in playing sports year-round, it was also mandatory for my kids to play sports.

This was our house—together. I assigned chores, but I always pitched in and did the work alongside them. Working together not only gave me an opportunity to praise them for a job well done, but it also provided a perfect time to discuss many subjects with them. Naturally, during this time, I developed my unique skill of giving them lectures. For the record, I called them discussions or lessons, but my children called them lectures. To honor them, let's just call them *Dad lectures* because that's probably how your child will see them too.

These lessons came after the slightest deviation from the established norm. If they did something I felt needed correcting, I simply gave a lecture about what had gone wrong. We also discussed how to correct it moving forward. It seems obvious that good parenting leads to good kids. Yet, for some reason, so many parents have difficulty. I can attest— these dad lectures work. My children proved to be excellent students with honor roll grades. Both eventually graduated from high school and college. After college, they both got jobs, got married, and ultimately had children of their own.

The genesis of this book came years later, after a visit to my daughter's home. At the time, her children were around ten years old. One of them did something wrong. My daughter sprang into action to correct his behavior. How did she do it? She lectured him. However, it wasn't just any lecture. It was one of mine—almost identical to what I had said to her years before. Sitting there in that moment, I was shocked and amazed. Dumbfounded! She really had heard and practically memorized my lectures.

For a while, I sat there quietly, reflecting on our discussions. At the time, I often thought she hadn't heard or even taken seriously a single word of what I said. I should have known. After a few years of talking to them, my children joked with me whenever I gave them one of my lectures. They claimed to have memorized all of them. They even numbered them. Without saying anything more, they sometimes jumped in to finish my sentences, saying exactly what I was about to say. These times ended in laughter and joking. That's why I always felt they hadn't taken our talks seriously.

This experience made me think about how vitally important what you say to kids is in the long run. They really do hear you. They remember everything—something that can be either good or bad based on what a parent consistently says to their children. That's why what you say really matters. Witnessing my daughter give one of my simply outstanding lectures to her son stirred old memories.

Her son, my grandson, had the exact reaction to her that my son always had to me. Strangely, he looked disinterested and bored, and I questioned whether he had even heard a word. Yet, I knew the answer was an emphatic yes! After watching the lecture right down to the challenge and the all-important hug, I realized it was not an accident that my grandchildren were also excellent students, active in sports, well liked, and had many friends. They were just like my children way back when.

Figuring things out wasn't easy, but over time, my parenting got better, and I also learned to end every lecture with three things: first, some humor; next, a challenge; and last, a hug. It seems that consistently correcting the little bad stuff very quickly meant the big, really bad stuff never happened.

My daughter used the same approach to parenting as me. My lectures became hers. She used them to cover crucial subjects with her kids. Most of my Dad lectures had nothing to do with schoolwork. It was the same for my daughter. Yet in her house, a new generation was doing what she and I once did. Using my proactive approach to parenting, she was developing successful, happy children—which I call victors, not victims.

In this book, I aspire to share my dad lectures along with their clue bird moments, and related stories to help bring these lessons to life. My hope is that other dads will see there really is an art and science to guiding a young person. I firmly believe the following lessons will benefit you, your children, grandchildren, and other family members you love.

THE CLUE BIRD

THE CLUE BIRD shows up in moments of trouble. Those very moments when timely, accurate, and helpful advice is needed because a quick decision must be made. A time when you can't be wrong. A time when a sudden and overwhelming feeling overcomes you. Perhaps it's a hunch about what to do.

It's compelling. You may hear a clear, concise voice that tells you just what you need to do. Imagine your house is on fire. You need to find your dog and get out. The next few moments are critical. You're suddenly on the clock. You get only one shot at this, and you can't afford to be wrong. So, it's no time for a mental debate, Zoom call, or group text. You just act on instinct, following your hunches—the advice you hear inside. That's the Clue Bird.

Throughout the years, I've asked many people to think back to a situation where they had to make a tough decision. I wondered if they felt an overwhelming mood change or if they heard a voice offering advice on what to do. It turns out, many people have had these exact experiences. You may have had them too. This is the advice of the Clue Bird. Although some may not consciously remember, I think many people have heard the Clue Bird. I also think sometimes it may simply be too noisy for some people to hear it.

Mostly, this mysterious, mystical little bird seems to be a compelling internal voice. My first encounter with the Clue Bird happened when I was in high school. I had a job as a dishwasher in a local restaurant. One night after closing, I couldn't get my motorcycle started. After trying for about half an hour, I realized it wasn't going to start.

Right then, my coworkers barged out of the restaurant. They offered me a ride home. I accepted, thinking I could come back the next day to fix my motorcycle in the daylight. It seemed like a promising idea. But just as I started to get into their car, a strange feeling swept over me. A little voice said, "Don't get in that car." So, I just stopped. I abruptly thanked them for their offer, saying I'd changed my mind. I told them I'd decided to call my brother to come pick me up because he might even have an idea about how to get the motorcycle started.

After leaving the restaurant, my coworkers had been hot-rodding their car as usual and ran a red light. They crashed into a crossing vehicle not too far from the parking lot. There were serious injuries that required hospitalization. I remember that night as if it happened yesterday.

Back home, safe in my room, I realized I'd experienced a curiously strange and seriously powerful hunch. I thought about how I had suddenly changed my mind. I knew there was no way I was getting into that car. That decision changed my life. My hunch was unexplainable—it came out of nowhere. It was simply an emphatic statement out of thin air. I had clearly heard it and accepted it on the spot. I became a believer that night.

My next encounter with this Clue Bird also occurred during my high school years. At the time, I had had serious stomach pain for several days. Trying to ignore it, I kept playing basketball, even though it got worse every day. It certainly didn't get better as I had hoped. On a beautiful, sunlit Friday morning, I rode my motorcycle to school as always, but I was hunched over with pain. Determined to get through the day, I went to class. During first period, the pain sent me to the nurse's station, where I asked if they could call my mother.

Predictably, the nurse questioned me. She probably figured if I had been healthy enough to ride my motorcycle to school, I must have just wanted to get out early on a sunny Friday. Not thinking me gravely ill, she said, "Maybe you could possibly return to class." I told her I couldn't, insisted I was sick, and then curled up on a cot to wait it out. After about an hour, the pain got worse—not better. With urgency, I asked her again to have someone pick me up. She finally complied.

Half an hour later, a strange lady came into the nurse's station, claiming I was, in fact, not her boy. The nurse had obviously called the wrong family. I confirmed my home phone number, and my mother was finally on the way. When she showed up, I overheard everything from the adjoining room. The head nurse suggested I was faking it.

She said my mother should just take me home, since I obviously wasn't going to any of my classes anyway. In the car, my mom yelled, "We're going home!" She asked what all the fuss was about. She didn't believe I was sick, since I'd played basketball the night before. Right then, a curious feeling came over me. I kept hearing the words, "Get to Dr. Sullivan's!"

Once again, I took that hunch and those words as the absolute truth. I told my mother we were, in fact, going to Dr. Sullivan's office because I was really, really sick. And then I threw up. At Dr. Sullivan's office, he told us I had appendicitis and sent us directly to St. Edwards Hospital. He closed his office and then met us there, where they removed my ruptured appendix.

Had we dragged it out by going home instead, it would only have gotten dangerously worse. That ended yet another encounter with this strange, overwhelming feeling, where I clearly heard a concise and definite statement that proved intuitive and helpful.

You know how it turned out when I listened to the Clue Bird. Now, let me share what happened when I chose to ignore his advice. At the time, I'd finished college and had just graduated from Officer Training School. Before entering flight school, I planned to go home to get married.

As I stepped onto the airliner, I had another curious sensation. An overwhelming feeling of dread came with the little voice in my head. Repeatedly, it said, "No, don't. No, don't." I knew deep in my bones exactly what the Clue Bird was talking about. His advice was an emphatic no! I thought, *what do I do now?*

They had planned the wedding, ordered the cake, and sent invitations. The grand event was on autopilot, so to speak. How could I be such a lousy human being by changing my mind or, even worse, being a no-show and causing a huge embarrassment and unnecessary expense to the families? I went home.

Certainly, I knew the Clue Bird's advice was correct, but I felt trapped. Being a young man, to my detriment, I just went along. Upon arrival, I met with several people. The happiness, revelry, and gifts overwhelmed me. Still, I had another personal moment with the Clue Bird.

Repeatedly, he said, "No, don't. No, don't." Privately, I fought back as hard as I could. Yet ultimately, I decided to ignore his sage-like advice. Advice that had never failed me. I decided to *press on*. To get married.

Finally, the wedding day came. The fuss and flurry of getting ready for the ceremony was almost chaotic. As I finished putting on my uniform, I was suddenly alone for a rare private moment. I took that moment to just sit down.

Instead of being joyful and happy, I felt overwhelmed with uneasiness and angst. My inner clue bird persisted in whispering, unmistakably: "No, don't. No, don't." With steadfast determination, or just being hardheaded, I convinced myself not to let any of these people down. I willed myself to *man up* and go through with it.

At the time, I believed it was just the well-known adage of having *cold feet*. Looking back, I sacrificed myself for the sake of the gathered assembly of friends and relatives. People who had come for *my wedding*, not theirs. I should have done exactly what the little bird said. I learned a life lesson the hard way. And I don't believe we need to learn things the hard way all the time. Perhaps never, if we learn to listen to the sage-like advice of the Clue Bird.

Let me share another interaction between me and the Clue Bird that happened when I was considering a major change in my employment. Back then, as a newly married man with a young child, like so many fathers, I realized for the first time in my life how my decisions didn't just impact me. They impacted my entire family.

That realization made the moment even harder. It marked a major step in both my personal and professional development. The decision itself was complicated. It meant giving up a great job I loved and was very good at to move across the country with my family.

It's always riskier to start over with a family—especially to take on a brand-new concept that could either be really good or really bad, with very little room in between. As always, I beat myself up for a good couple of weeks, like most new dads might.

I went back and forth, vacillating between staying where I was and taking this new opportunity. To decide, I used the Benjamin Franklin T-sheet of pros and cons, threw darts, met with friends, took long walks, and even played on my Ouija board. Still, I was on the fence. As decision time approached, I kept thinking: If I say no and it turns out to be a tremendous success, I'll feel awful. But if the project is doomed from the start, staying where I am will make me look like a genius for the very first time in my life.

Well, the final night came. I had made the decision: I was going to stay in my current job and graciously decline their offer when they called the next morning. But strangely, while I talked to them an overwhelming sensation came over me. I heard the now-familiar voice say, clear as day: "I accept, and thank you for this opportunity for all of us."

Without even thinking, I blurted out exactly what the Clue Bird had just said. After an hour of congratulations and camaraderie, I hung up the phone. I couldn't believe what I had just done. And now, looking back, I have to say, without hesitation: taking that opportunity was in fact the best decision I ever made.

The Clue Bird was spot on and sage-like. I can recall countless decisions, some life-or-death situations, while others were just simple, *which road should I take* kind of things. No matter how complex the issue, that ole familiar feeling would suddenly overtake me, and then I'd hear that little voice with complete clarity. I've learned the hard way to always take his advice. It has made my life easier by helping me avoid some would-be mistakes. Don't we all want that for ourselves and our children?

Years ago, a friend told me about driving down the freeway one afternoon, with thunderstorms and tornadoes sweeping through the area, when suddenly, a funnel cloud appeared on the freeway right in front of him. He sensed the danger immediately. Thinking about cutting through the median, he feared getting stuck because it looked very wet and muddy.

Surprisingly, the tornado got remarkably close, forcing him to pull off the highway. In a noticeably clear instant, he heard, "Get in the ditch." He got out of the car, ran to a ditch, and laid down. Half submerged in muddy water, wearing a brand-new suit, he stayed there until the tornado passed. Later, he told me he would never have thought to do that, but it came to him as a clear and concise command. Following it to the letter may have saved his life.

Another friend has a similar story. On his way home from a business dinner, he realized he was extremely low on gas. He decided to stop at the next gas station. But as he approached, an overwhelming feeling overtook him.

Right then, he curiously heard the soft-spoken words, "Don't stop. Keep moving." He didn't stop. For unexplainable reasons, he pushed on the gas. Later that evening, while watching the news, he sat in disbelief. A live feed ran the story about an attempted robbery and hostage situation in progress at that very gas station.

The above stories are about everyday people. But what about professions like firefighters, fighter pilots, and soldiers? These are professions where people regularly encounter the Clue Bird. Many times, in fighter squadrons during post-flight debriefings, pilots sometimes discuss unusual experiences. Maybe it was an in-flight emergency that got safely resolved. Someone might shout out to the pilot, "Did the Clue Bird land on your shoulder and give you some useful advice?"

That question was often met with a chorus of laughter. Usually, that pilot had just dealt with a real emergency where he experienced a curious but welcome mental clarity while under tremendous pressure to get things right on the first try. In such cases, the Clue Bird's advice likely saved lives.

I suspect many firefighters encounter the Clue Bird in smoky, dangerous situations. They might turn left or right, stop, or go down one hallway instead of another. Certainly, firefighters rely on their training and personal fitness first. Yet sometimes they get hunches that save them and others. In a debriefing, a firefighter might say he didn't know precisely why he acted a certain way, but his decision proved exceptionally brilliant. And it happens more often than not.

Consider police officers. They perform at extraordinary levels thanks to their excellent training, fitness, and professionalism. Still, they often face highly complex, fast-changing situations. Right in front of them, events unfold at warp speed. And they make astonishingly quick and accurate decisions based on a hunch or a feeling that had to come from somewhere.

Like firefighters and police officers, soldiers benefit from the Clue Bird too. They rely on their training and personal fitness to operate in diverse environments. They follow a chain of command and adhere to it as part of their duty. But in the fog of war, when lives are on the line amid the chaos, survival then depends on split-second decisions. How often do they feel a hunch about where to go next? Do we stop, or do we press the attack?

Sometimes, we don't know what to do when confronted with a weighty decision. We might seek the advice of counsel, friends, relatives, coworkers, or even our pet cat. But like with my wedding decision, my choices only affected me—not those who chimed in with free advice.

The ultimate decisions we make when faced with problems or issues are ours and ours alone. So is the life we experience because of them. Often, the clarity of a sage-like hunch can be brilliant. You just go with your gut. It's like getting a text message from your Clue Bird, about what to do. I believe we all have a Clue Bird in us. He whispers sage-like advice into our ears, whether we know it or not.

In my life, there have been thirteen important Clue Bird experiences I'd like to share in this book. These discussions deal with problems we've all faced growing up. Maybe even the very same problems our parents had to confront. Life lessons, in a strange way, are universal. They never change from generation to generation.

Fortunately, the Clue Bird has provided answers to help confront the problems of growing up. My hope is that these Clue Bird lessons will help parents guide and teach their children these valuable life lessons.

You, Inc.

THERE IS NO BETTER way to build a solid foundation than to teach children to care about who they are and who they want to become in the future. The business of being you is an all-day, everyday job. From the beginning—ideally, as early as possible—we should all see ourselves not only as a person but as an actual corporation too. Let's call it *You, Inc.* And you? You are its President.

As President, you're responsible for the smooth operation and growth of your company. You must ensure your company offers great products, operates fairly, remains successful, is a good neighbor, serves its community, and does charity work. Running *You, Inc.* this way would make anyone proud.

As a parent, when you run your company with integrity and purpose, you teach your children to do the same. It starts in childhood. Yes, every child wants to stay a child and do whatever they want, whenever they want, having their mom's and dad's take care of everything. But if children don't learn to see themselves as their own President, they may refuse to grow up even as their bodies mature. Eventually, something has to give. Luckily, most young people eventually give up being kids so they can get on with life.

You want to make sure your children have command of themselves—to act as President of their very own *You, Inc.* Parents who aren't the President of themselves raise children who turn out the same way. This is not good. These types of children don't give up being a kid. They mismanage their lives.

When this happens, others may need to take over the role of managing the child's *You, Inc.* If not a parent or relative, it could be something worse—like the legal system. That's why this concept is foundational to the lectures in this book. We'll return to *You, Inc.* again and again to explore how parents can help their children build the healthiest, most productive corporation possible.

Everyone should be their own President. As President of *You, Inc.*, doing what you want to do first and not doing what you should is irresponsible. It never ends well. Do you want your child to lose their job as President? Of course not. But if parents fail dismally at this job, someone or something will take over. The kid gets fired.

Depending on the situation, a parent, relative, juvenile detention, jail, or prison steps in. To keep the job of President, children must learn to master doing what they want to do only after doing what they should do. What's the definition of a wonderful life? It's blending responsibility with enjoyment. As a proactive parent, you must help your children commit to doing what they should do first, not just what feels good in the moment.

Every now and again, go right up to your children and ask, "How is *You, Inc.* doing with you as its president? Are you proud of what you've accomplished?" Keep the conversation going. Find out if they're tracking where they are and where they thought they'd be at this point in their growth.

Get them thinking about whether they feel behind or ahead in the game of life. Give them space to talk about how they see their role as a community partner. Wrap up with a discussion on how they might improve their performance, including specifics about how they plan to keep their job as President of their *You, Inc.*

These discussions help young people reflect. Using my own life as a reference, I'd honestly say, at first I headed down the road as a lousy president of me. I was miserable. I only did schoolwork when I could because I worked to help the family. But something changed. I took control, thanks to the Clue Bird's advice. Over time, I became a quality President of my own *You, Inc.*

Not having a father meant learning to see myself on my own, without that kind of guidance. For parents reading this book, it's not too late to encourage your child to be the President of themselves. With your help, they won't become lousy Presidents.

Remember, everything has a certain minimum expectation. In school, it's outlined in the syllabus—it's the bare minimum the course requires. But do you want your child to strive for the minimum? No! You don't ever want them to seek only what's absolutely necessary just to get by. Running *You, Inc.* takes effort. That means a lot of hard work. Parents must teach this early. If they don't, their child may grow into a minimum-effort adult.

Everyone hopes to achieve their goals and dreams. Sadly, many never do. But by learning to manage your life like a business, you can reach your later years both comfortable and satisfied. Doing this backward, by taking life easy as a young person, may mean arriving at middle age or beyond without energy, good health, or assets. If this happens, your life might not only be difficult, but you may also spend your later years regretting how little you did with it.

You Inc. is not optional. It's real—and already happening, whether people take care of it or not. The key is parents. They must impart two things to their kids. First, help them become their own best friend for life.

Second, show them how to become self-sufficient. The best way to do this is to dream often, dream big, and then work like you're possessed. That way, as you age, you can slow down and enjoy the rewards of a life well lived. This is what every child must know. With a parent's help, children can build a *You, Inc.* that makes them proud. One that pays them back as they age and lets them live their best life.

Now that you know what *You, Inc.* is all about, remember this concept is foundational to every topic in this book. As we look at the issues, many of which you may have faced yourself, let them serve as a guide. By following the Clue Bird's advice, you can help your child navigate their personal journey as they build a *You, Inc.* from the ground up. With your guidance, they will keep the job as its president.

To begin, we'll talk about the foundational five spokes of a balanced life to ensure they're fit to lead *You, Inc.* Then, we'll explore what leadership really means. From there, we'll tackle how to face problems as options, so your child doesn't get stuck or feel helpless. Finally, we'll delve into the details of how kids can reach their dreams through hard work, mental preparation, practice, and planning.

Ultimately, managing *You, Inc.* is about the pursuit of excellence. Anyone can do it. But the road stays much smoother when parents start early and show their child how to manage and run their very own *You, Inc.* It helps them win their battle to become victors.

THE FIVE SPOKES

THERE ARE FIVE basic categories that make up the Wheel of Life (WOL): love, personal, family, spiritual, and physical. They represent our inner qualities. The stuff that ensures we become permanent leaders of ourselves, and eventually of others. They help us build a strong *You, Inc.* Imagine them as a spoke on a wheel, where each spoke represents you from birth to death.

When we were born, our spokes were short and even in length, making our WOL small but very round. As we grow, our spokes also grow. Hopefully, our wheel stays round. When someone's WOL grows evenly, it means they've spent equal time and effort on each spoke, letting their wheel of life grow larger. In this case, their life continues to simply roll along smoothly and effortlessly.

If, however, the focus since birth stays on just one or two spokes, those spokes grow longer than the rest. The neglected spokes don't grow. As a result, your WOL gets out of round or oblong. It can't roll smoothly. Life then seems painful, difficult, and progress becomes nearly impossible. That's why it's important for parents to insist their children work on all aspects of their lives. It's the only way for the spokes to grow evenly.

The following discussion covers the core spokes on our WOL. Cultivating them brings balance to our lives and helps us make sure children stay in balance, too.

Love

First of all, you must love yourself. Always be your own best friend. Never let yourself down. That means keeping the promises you make to yourself. Always. No matter what. We all know from experience how empty it feels when someone lets you down or doesn't keep their word. So how much worse is it when you betray yourself? That feeling is why and how so many people come to hate themselves. You discount you, making yourself small and meaningless. You do it to yourself. So, remember to honor yourself first, and don't ever, ever break a promise you made to yourself. No matter how trivial that promise—keep it.

Let's say you promised yourself to work out at a gym three times a week until you changed your mind. That's great. If you didn't work out, it really wouldn't matter—but that's not the point. You promised yourself, but you didn't go to the gym. That is the core problem.

It's not muscle development. It's the mental and emotional void of letting yourself down. In life, you should be the last person on earth to let yourself down. If you can't count on yourself, who else can you trust to not let you down? Going to the gym three times per week as promised would have grown muscle and that would be fine, but more importantly, your love and respect for yourself would have grown too.

Self-leadership is essential to self-love. It sets you up for a successful lifetime of being your own best friend. This starts by choosing what's best for you and what's important to you, while honoring every promise you make to yourself. It's much better than living a whimsical life, of mostly just doing what you feel like doing at any particular time, with no plan or agenda. Loving yourself takes work. It means not doing just whatever comes along or going along with whatever your friends want to do.

First, let's define *friend*. Webster's Dictionary defines friend as "a person whom one knows well and is fond of, an ally, supporter, and sympathizer." When we first start making friends, they're often random people who happen to be in our family, school, or church. If you suddenly found a new job in another city, your children would be in a new school, meeting yet another pool of random people to practice their social skills with.

I remember my children telling me just how important their friends were to them. I told them most of those friendships were the result of random chance. I'd tell them that after graduating, they'd probably never see those classmates again—except maybe at a class reunion.

I emphasized balance. I wanted my kids to know their friends were important—but not so important that they should go along with the crowd or do something harmful they'd regret. I insisted my kids honor their friends but also remember to love themselves by always being true to their best friend—themselves. I also asked them to think about why they formed friendships with only a few people at their school. That old adage, "Show me your friends and I'll show you who you are," is very true.

Your choice of friends defines you, and so does your child's. Teach them to make sure their choices say, *I love myself*. Remind them they're an eternal spirit in a born-to-die body—not a body with a spirit. Since the essence of you is a birthless, deathless, perfect spirit attached to your physical body, it's easy to love yourself. Always, in every way, love yourself.

Personal

On a personal level, consider what is best for *You, Inc.* Acting as its president, be responsible for managing yourself as if you are a company. Let your decisions be matter-of-fact, black and white, and focused on doing what's best to make your company strong, prosperous, and growing. Some of these include hygiene, sleep, nourishment, and personal property. All of these connect to emotional well-being and personal growth. It's why you ensure your child goes to bed on time, eats nutritious food, and learns to control themselves.

For all of us, this job first belonged to our parents but gradually shifted to us. We all had to learn to set and honor limits. For children, especially teens, this means limiting cellphone usage, TV time, and gameplay. This is better than allowing unlimited screen time. For a good life, maintaining a healthy weight, spending time with siblings and family pets, doing chores, and helping a neighbor are good daily responsibilities.

On a personal level, setting performance standards and goals to consistently honor themselves will maximize balanced growth every day of every year moving forward. Again, have your child make a primary agreement with themselves to honor a promise to care for themselves—no matter what.

Family

You are a member of many families. The one you physically live with is just one of them. Everyone should promise to always do what is best for this relationship—not just what feels best or what they can simply get away with doing. Promise to be dependable, as an honorable father, mother, son, or daughter. Always do what's best without having to be asked. Without fail, make a promise to you and only you. Never break it, no matter how you feel at the time.

Insist that older children support their siblings. They can help their brothers or sisters who are going down a trail they've already blazed. They can be a leader to them as well as act as intermediaries between siblings and caregivers. Have them promise to protect and guide the younger ones with kindness and love, regardless of how they feel about them in the moment.

Teach kids to overlook the faults they see in their siblings. Older children should know their support, advice, and guidance can make a lasting impact, helping their younger brothers and sisters outgrow shortcomings. Remember, you probably acted just like, or even worse than, your kids. Don't have a short memory when dealing with your children, and they won't have one when dealing with each other or with you.

Don't judge them or anyone. Only judge yourself. Make sure older siblings take on the responsibility of loving, protecting, coaching, and guiding those behind them in age, steering them away from needless mistakes. It will make their journeys easier. Oftentimes, teaching someone else makes you better too, because you really learn something when you teach it.

Help your child strive to exceed expectations. Let them learn to be the gift in the room. When they are... their siblings and yes, even the dog, will look up to them and want to emulate them.

Physical

What is growing up? It's having a physical body on autopilot. Every child grows physically, like it or not. The body grows and matures, even without enough sleep, good hygiene, a healthy diet, or freedom from drugs and alcohol. But when not in balance, problems crop up. The secret is to match automatic physical growth with not-so-automatic emotional and mental growth.

That's what parents must prepare them to do. Herein lies the problem with most people: they really don't want to grow up. They want to stay kids forever, having others take care of them, or letting them roam around aimlessly to childishly do whatever they want to do—never what they need to do.

Our job as parents is to guide our children's mental and emotional growth. After that, the child can take over by matching their mental and emotional growth to their physical growth to achieve balance.

Spiritual

Consider the idea that we are a spirit in a body—not a body in a spirit. What does this realization mean? What if we're a birthless, deathless, perfect spirit? Wouldn't that make it easier to love ourselves and others? Realizing you are an amazing spirit puts you in a different position when you evaluate yourself.

Knowing you're an entity of wonder lessens the need or desire to criticize or demean yourself or others. It can create an opening to take the high road—not only with ourselves, but with our children. As children, we learn pertinent moral lessons, but do we always strive to live by them? Realizing we're spiritual beings might make it easier to live by a higher standard.

As president of *You, Inc.*, you can be honorable to yourself, living up to those high standards every moment. Treat yourself as you would your best friend. Make promises to yourself and never cheat by not honoring those promises. How will your child learn to be spiritually balanced if you, their parent, can't do it? Let's teach children to treat themselves and others as if they're each a perfectly made spirit and to be the gift in the room.

The five spokes addressed here are crucial to get your children off to a good start. You can add spokes as they grow to populate their WOL based on new interests that will certainly pop up in their journeys. Parents must stay balanced too, because when they do, it shows their children how to do it. As your children grow, take time to teach them how to deal with the challenging life experiences they face. Teach them the importance of caring for their WOL, which keeps them "in the round," so to speak.

THE WHEEL OF LIFE
(FIVE BASIC CATEGORIES)

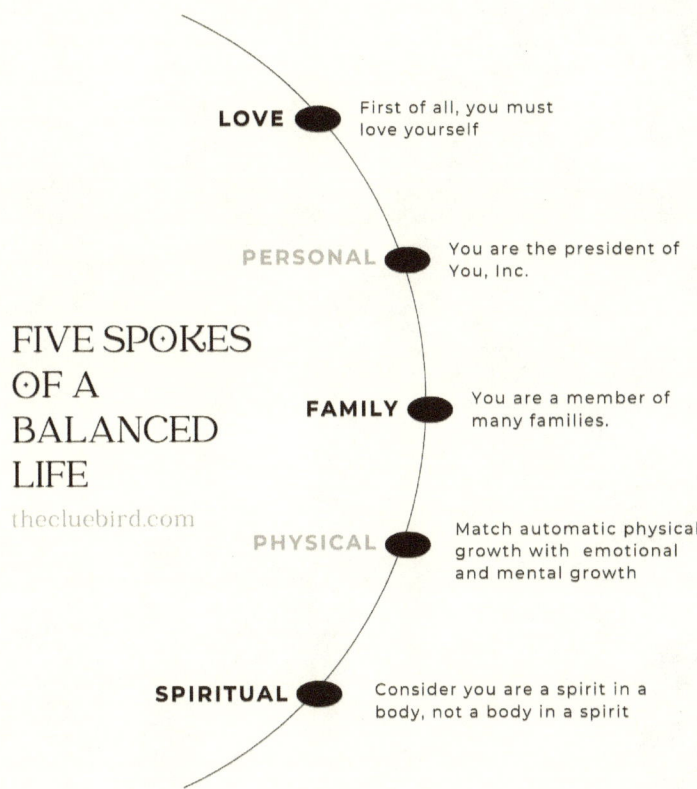

FIVE SPOKES OF A BALANCED LIFE

thecluebird.com

LOVE — First of all, you must love yourself

PERSONAL — You are the president of You, Inc.

FAMILY — You are a member of many families.

PHYSICAL — Match automatic physical growth with emotional and mental growth

SPIRITUAL — Consider you are a spirit in a body, not a body in a spirit

Each spoke represents a part of your life, from birth to death.

LESSON 1

LEADERSHIP BEGINS WITH YOU

LEADERSHIP IS SOMETHING we should discuss with children at an early age. It's not that hard. The challenge is transferring responsibility early by letting children do the things they can do for themselves. It's a balancing act. Kids want to remain kids but we can't allow that. By transferring the things they can do for themselves, parents ensure their children become responsible adults. In the *You, Inc.* chapter, we addressed teaching children to think of themselves as a company. That viewpoint is the beginning of helping a child learn to lead themselves.

I often wonder what keeps young American suburbanites from relentlessly pursuing their dreams—not a casual pursuit, but with that *do-or-die* effort people with much less seem to have. Why do children go down the wrong path in life? Why do we struggle to get children to live up to their potential?

It's worse when children end up with others taking care of them because of their bad choices. In stark contrast, the meek, the poor, and the needy, are often more driven. They use their imaginations to dream about what can be. They visualize themselves as who they want to become, not as who they are in their present state.

When it came to having the finer things in life, my family wasn't exactly a potential candidate. In fact, we were firmly planted on the wrong side of the economic tracks. We struggled to keep up, which forced most of the kids to drop out of school and start working at the first opportunity. Everyone had to get menial jobs to help the family finances. As a family, we punished each generation of our kids by taking them out of school early. Lack of education held us back. We couldn't move forward or advance economically. It was a vicious cycle.

One night, I remember working to exhaustion. I was hungry and tired but needed to get my homework done under the bare light bulb hanging by a wire from the ceiling. Exhausted, I put my head on my books and fell asleep. Stirred awake, I could swear I saw a beautiful little bird. I heard, "First become a leader of yourself and then be a leader of others." Startled, I sat up in that small living room. The light was still on. I thought about those words. Somehow, I knew—deep down— what the little bird had said was eerily true.

In a moment, I committed myself to understanding what this message was about. I was determined to make sense of the first part of the message: "First become a leader of yourself." I realized I was not much of a leader. I was a kid from a struggling family, sometimes doing what I was told and exerting minimum effort with my schoolwork.

I blamed being tired for my lack of academic success. Yet I also spent a lot of my time feeling sorry for myself and being jealous of my school friends who had more than we did. I understood I needed to learn about leadership if I wanted to become a leader of myself, as the Clue Bird had suggested. I figured becoming a leader was my way out of the cycle of being poor.

Deciphering the message

My grandpa fought in the war and learned about leadership from his time in the military. I had great regard for my grandfather and went to him for advice. He explained how he counted on his leaders to be "squared away." In the military, a "squared away soldier" is always prepared. With these soldiers, nothing is missed or left undone.

They are ready. Grandpa said, "All of us soldiers could count on them to help us out because they had everything covered." They were the soldiers who got promoted and placed in positions of leadership because everyone trusted them. People like my grandpa willingly followed them. He said those soldiers could lead other men because they earned it by first being leaders of themselves.

Smiling, his next comment to me was: "To become a leader, treat yourself like you would your best friend." He told me to become my best friend by learning to love and forgive myself. He said that before anything else, I had to develop personal leadership skills because it was the first step to earning the right to lead others. I didn't have a clue. He believed kids typically operate with their physical bodies in charge of them. Looking at me, he said that's why I only did what I wanted to do. He made it clear I was a whimsical kid, driven by getting what I wanted without concern for what I needed to do.

According to my grandpa, the formula to become a leader of men was learning to lead yourself, putting your mind in charge of your body, and being *squared away*. He believed this was what it took to *become a leader of men*. From grandpa, I came to understand that I had to be in charge of me and my body in order to earn the right to lead others. Sitting with him, I came to see how I behaved like an irrational actor, doing the minimum at the last possible moment.

Although I didn't agree, he thought I wanted others to do the things I could do for myself. Thinking it through for a minute made me feel guilty because he had described me perfectly. My grandfather told me to become a leader of myself by deciding to put my mind in charge of me. Although it came later in life, he was telling me how to become the president of me—how to grow my own *You, Inc.*

It meant I had to make promises to myself and then never break them. Right then, I had to start living, trusting, and honoring myself. I had to be my new best friend. With great resolve, I would need to dominate my body, along with its whimsical wants, to make it subservient to my mind. My mind had to call the shots. My mind had to decide that I would no longer do the minimum. After talking with my grandfather, I learned it was my job to do what I must do before thinking about what I might want to do.

That day, I started putting my mind in charge to make me a rational actor who stayed in control of me. Once I got my mind in charge of calling the shots, I could no longer be a minimal-effort person. Suddenly, I morphed into a maximum-effort person. I became an early, first-in-line, barrier-breaking, *hair-on-fire* type of person. I was finally ready to lead others. This is personal leadership. This is holy ground where few people walk.

Applying the message

I began to set goals with my mind in charge. My mind dictated how I could consistently act like a person possessed in pursuit of achieving my goals. This is what we want for kids. Nothing less. Lift the people you are leading. Start with your own children. When a parent fails to show their child how to lead themselves, they prevent them from earning the right to lead others. When children decide to lead themselves, they earn the right. That's why children must strive to be excellent at everything they do.

An example of this phenomenon is playing a sport with players who are far better than you. Have you ever done that? If you have, I'll bet you played your best while playing with them. People don't turn their backs on excellence. Excellent leaders set a high bar for others to follow—not the other way around.

Over the years, I employed teens and young adults who were still in high school or college. Some were moonlighting. During their breaks, I'd go out to thank them for their hard work. Eventually, we'd cut up a little, joke around, and laugh about something that had happened earlier. Sometimes, I asked them about their hopes, dreams, or where they saw themselves in ten years. The answers astonished me.

Sadly, most didn't have any hopes, dreams, or future plans. It struck me that they were just existing and growing old. In contrast, my children, who were of the same age, had hopes, dreams, and ambitious plans for themselves.

Working on leadership development with my kids was a useful way to help them put their minds in charge of their bodies. It's the first step to becoming a leader of yourself. At work, I would randomly assign an employee to supervise a small group of co-workers for a shift. Later, I'd correct any mistakes I noticed and praise them for a job well done. At home, I did the same.

For example, I'd put one of my kids in charge of the yard work for the day. They could assign specific chores to any of us. When we finished, I'd offer a list of probable improvements and praise them for their hard work. To develop leadership skills in your kids, set up situations like these and put them in charge. It gives them a safe way to experience leadership, build confidence, and reassure parents that their kids will turn out just fine.

Please note, there's a huge difference between being a leader and being in charge. Let's say you work for a big company and have a mean boss. They yell, get angry, throw stuff—the whole bit. The employees have no respect for them; they simply put up with the behavior. That's not true leadership. True leaders are humble, approachable, and self-deprecating.

They're comfortable in their own skin because they are in charge of themselves. Those qualities allow them to lead others. They become humble and confident leaders who never forget where they came from. It makes them approachable because real leaders lift others up. They never put people down.

True leaders help their people grow—and cheer when they rise. They build relationships rooted in mutual trust. Leaders can ask their people questions, and their people can openly ask questions of them. Both sides can rely on getting real, honest answers from each other. True leaders know they're in charge. They don't have to prove it to anyone. They lead by being truthful, honest, and respectful with their employees.

Raising my children, I struggled to balance not spoiling them with keeping them focused on achieving their own hopes and dreams. Having them think in terms of being president of *You, Inc.* changed their viewpoint. They shifted perspective from just being kids to being in charge of themselves. People don't just follow excellent leaders. What they do is try to emulate them by changing their own behavior. Leadership is contagious. Everyone in a room can spot the leader. What will your child be?

Leadership in action

There's a story I'll never forget about soldiers landing on a hostile shore. They rode in rafts at night, quietly approaching an island held by the enemy. The enemy not only occupied the island but were also dug in and heavily fortified. They were a notorious lot with a reputation for being highly skilled and ruthless fighters. *This will not be an easy night*, thought the commander of the invading force. After successfully landing, the soldiers prepared to march into the inevitable battle.

Yet before departing, the commander gave a shocking order: burn the boats. Reluctantly, the men obeyed. They burned each and every boat. There was no way to escape. If the ensuing fight didn't go well, they would all perish. Each man, on his most personal level, knew it. As comrades in arms, they hustled into the night—to either do or die. Leadership at its finest.

Take a moment to visualize yourself in a situation where you're in charge of a group of soldiers in a combat zone. Per your orders, it's time to storm the hill covered with enemy troops. It means soldiers will be injured or even killed. You love these guys for what you've been through together. Then it's time for you to say, "Gentlemen, let's go!" Do your children have that kind of leadership, courage, and commitment to operate in such an environment? If not, they have a long way to go. To help them, talk about the ideas my grandpa shared about leadership. His advice changed my life, and I remain forever grateful.

Since the founding of our country, dreamers and the downtrodden have steadily arrived at our shores, believing that if they got here, they could achieve their dreams. For them, our country is free from oppression—unlike any place else on Earth. Others risk their lives to get here and ultimately succeed, starting with much less than some American children. They master taking charge of their lives. For the children of well-off parents, perhaps the need to achieve is not as important. They think, *I already have it made.*

We should encourage every child, even those born on the right side of the tracks, as the saying goes, to pursue excellence in their lives. This pursuit begins with teaching children about leadership, as it will change them in a positive way. The meek, or poor, like me and others back when I was a teenager, had hopes and dreams.

We would tell each other what we were going to become someday. We used our imaginations to conjure up what we most desired. With focus and maximum effort, we set out to achieve our dreams. Like me, many of us became the very people we wanted to become. Yet it seems some who grow up with abundance don't have a need to dream big.

That's why the sooner you start leadership development with your children, the more likely they'll be able to achieve their dreams too.

The Clue Bird's suggestion, *"First become a leader of yourself and then become a leader of others,"* is spot on. It proves beneficial in bringing up children to lead themselves first. They learn to do what they must do first. It means developing self-control and effort-based habits.

Whether rich or poor, such children take a positive step by morphing into maximum-effort kids. To get there, parents must talk with their children about dreaming big and setting goals. Over time, they will achieve those goals. Having command of themselves is a great foundation for slowly earning the right to lead others. Maybe someday, with a little dreaming, your children could become like the leader who ordered his men to burn their boats. The world awaits.

First become a leader of yourself and then become a leader of others.

1- Be your best friend. Learn to love and forgive yourself.

2- Put your mind in charge of you. Avoid being a whimsical, irrational actor driven mostly by your physical desires.

3- Leading others is earned by first becoming a leader of yourself.

4- True leaders are humble, approachable and self-depreciating. They know they're in charge and don't have to prove it.

5- Being in charge of *You, Inc.*, means setting goals, hard work and doing what you must do first.

Lesson 2

Problems or Options

From birth until death, we all face what we call problems. Dealing with problems is part of life—everyone has them. That's why we need to start teaching problem management early. It proactively prepares children to deal with life. Anyone can become frustrated and overwhelmed when improperly dealing with problems. Parents must diligently monitor their children for signs of poor problem management. Isolation, anger, and poor performance are common signs indicating that a child needs help. Never overlook the signs. If left unresolved, these issues can lead to failure in many areas—possibly even mental and physical illness.

Children watch the people around them. They especially listen to and observe what their parents say and do. We may think children don't hear a word we say, but that's simply incorrect. Prove it to yourself by looking back on your childhood. Remember how you were as a kid? What's important to note is that children mirror what they see or hear in their homes. This can be both good and bad.

When parents don't appear visibly shaken, upset, or obsessed over their problems, children learn to keep their problems manageable as well. However, in households that do the opposite, the constant nag of worry can escalate to anger. Seeing such behavior will cause some children to act likewise.

Looking back at my household growing up, we were in the group that poorly dealt with problems. There were a host of issues. I grew up in an economically poor household, had no dad in my life, and lived with my grandmother and her many children. We lived in an old two-story wooden house in a rural setting, with a coal-burning potbelly stove in the living room. There wasn't enough money, but still a lot of mouths to feed. Consider November in the Midwest with an often empty coal bin—freezing. Making ends meet wasn't easy. Everyone in the family attended elementary school until about the fifth or sixth grade, quit to find a job, and then helped with the family finances.

Some family members lived at Grandma's house long past the age when they should have moved out. They simply couldn't afford to step out on their own. Leaving school early to get a job really set everyone back economically. As a young boy, I witnessed the adults at home talking into the wee hours.

Night after night, I listened to them sitting around, complaining about their mounting problems. Maybe someone got laid off, another was already unemployed, or a car wouldn't start. With no money for repairs, someone was now walking to work. Someone was sick, but we couldn't afford a doctor's visit. We were out of coal. And every so often, yet another long-lost relative with his wife and kids in tow, would show up in the middle of the night, in dire straits, and needing a place to stay. My family stayed angry, afraid, and helpless.

Listening to the problems all around me, I slowly but surely integrated what I heard. Scarcity, hopelessness, sickness, pain, and suffering had all been caused by their mountain of problems. Problems that would never get any better. This way of thinking burned into my brain. Sadly, I became just like them.

Slowly but predictably, what I had learned came to fruition: things weren't going well for me in high school. I was miserable with an enormous stack of problems. I struggled academically, had only a few friends, and wanted to play many sports but got cut trying out for most of them. Unfortunately, my few friends acted just like me. Nothing seemed to work in my life. I began to feel the need to quit school, get a job, and move on.

One night, worrying about everything in my miserable, lonely life, I failed to do my homework. Frustrated and angry, I went to bed. While asleep, I had a dream—not just any dream, but one in color. It was so vivid that I felt I could reach out and touch the little bird that came to me. A beautiful red bird stood there, looking directly at me while saying, "Is it a problem, or is it just an option? So, deal with it and relax." Normally, I would've ignored the dream and gotten busy worrying about this problem or that one out of habit, but this dream felt too real to ignore.

I repeated what the little bird had said out loud many times so I wouldn't forget. I even wrote those words down on a piece of scrap paper. I still have it. This encounter felt as real as the message itself. There was just something that rang true about the simple statement, though I couldn't figure it out. Deep down, I knew I needed help on many levels. I wanted to discuss this dream, but only with someone outside of my family to avoid the predictable laughter and subsequent humiliation. I decided to start with my math teacher, Mrs. Wilson, because I had a high regard for her.

Deciphering the message

In Mrs. Wilson's classroom, I apologetically asked to discuss a matter not related to math class. She smiled and said we could talk right then because her next meeting had just been canceled. Before a word was spoken, she unexpectedly told me she had a high regard for me. She believed I could be an excellent student and should do well in life. It was the best compliment I'd ever received. It was priceless to me.

Wiping away a tear, I suddenly felt like exploding with pride for the first time in my life. Getting right to it, I asked, "Do you know what... *Is it a problem or is it just an option? So, deal with it and relax*, might mean?" Curiously, she smiled again as if she had heard this exact question from other students. After careful thought, she suggested we break the statement down into two parts before analyzing it.

We addressed "Is it a problem or is it just an option?" first. Mrs. Wilson suggested we fully define the word *problem* to accurately describe it. While pulling out her heavily used dictionary, she explained how the word problem is often misused. She then summarized the definition of problem as "a perplexing or difficult matter, person, and more."

Further, *perplexing* meant to "make a person uncertain, doubtful, and more confused." She explained how people often, without any thought, mislabel unpleasant issues in their lives as problems. Everything becomes a problem.

She thought calling something a problem makes any issue seem much bigger and more unsolvable than it really is. We talked about how people often label unpleasant things as problems because that's what they learned to do growing up. Teaching math had taught her a lot about frustration. First off, she believed calling something a problem causes people to feel overwhelmed, inadequate, and filled with angst. I quietly agreed because she had just described my home life. It finally made sense why my family so often felt overwhelmed and inadequate.

For the first time, sitting with Mrs. Wilson, I came to see how mislabeling something as a problem is a major mistake. It's making a mountain out of a molehill. I shared how everyone endlessly discussing problems felt like hearing several broken records playing all at once. It finally became clear how crippling it was.

We kept ourselves in a horrible mental box, believing we couldn't remove problems from our lives. No one ever thought to offer up solutions to keep us from feeling helpless. That's why the way we dealt with things never made us feel good. We just had a pile of insurmountable issues, felt helpless, and couldn't rid ourselves of them.

Mrs. Wilson helped me see how very few real problems there are in our lives. She asked, "What should we more accurately call all of the unpleasant issues we face?" The answer was in the Clue Bird's statement: "Or is it just an option?" We then looked up the word *option* together. It's defined as "a choosing, a choice, something that is or can be chosen." The Clue Bird's use of the word just perfectly describes the true order of importance between a real problem and an option.

As I sat there digesting the conversation, I suddenly felt lighter. It was simple. A real problem is a life-changing, permanent setback. When a real problem hits, whatever happens moving forward, a person's life will never be the same. In contrast, an option means having a choice—a way to eliminate an unpleasant issue.

That's why most unpleasant issues are not problems at all. They're just options. I realized most of the unwanted issues I'd face in my life would be just that: options or choices. *I'm not helpless! I'm in charge of my life,* I told myself. Right then, I experienced a new feeling of being powerful. *Life isn't so hard after all,* I thought. I sat there wishing someone had told me years earlier. Although I regretted not having learned it as a child, I knew this shift to view problems as options would help me eliminate my unpleasant issues.

Without proper coaching, like so many children, I needlessly went through mental torment. Thankfully, Mrs. Wilson continued, saying the good news is... we luckily have very few real problems to deal with— maybe in our entire lifetimes. Real problems are rare. People such as Tony Robbins say your life changes in a moment. It might take years to get there, but it changes in a moment. Real problems are life changers. Terminal illness, serious accidents, wars, and natural disasters are examples of real problems.

No matter what we do to resolve a real problem, we are forever changed—perhaps worse off. But if the unwanted issue is just an option, it's possible to simply sit down by yourself or with trusted friends or family to compile a list of options.

Applying the message

The last part of the statement, "and relax," is important too. Mrs. Wilson said not to overlook it. "So, deal with it and relax" is self-explanatory. It means deciding how to correctly label what you're confronted with. All I needed to do was follow what the Clue Bird said to get things done. I finished my conversation with Mrs. Wilson and thanked her for her time. After leaving, I sat alone in an empty classroom, frantically writing down everything I could recall from our meeting, afraid I'd forget something important. After that, it only took me a couple of hours to list everything I considered an unwanted issue.

The list amazed me because I could see how many of the issues were caused by me to begin with. It hit me hard. Sitting there, I decided that if I created these issues, then surely I could get rid of them. For each one, I drew up a list of workable solutions and picked the best option to move forward. That was step one: identifying the possible courses of action to eliminate each issue.

Mrs. Wilson had said, "With a list of options, you simply pick the obvious best choice out of the bunch and then wholeheartedly commit to implementing it into your life." She promised that if I worked this process, I'd see those negative issues diminish and my quality of life improve. Once I was done, I felt unburdened.

Knowing about problems or options was about to make my life vastly different. I wouldn't have to spend another minute in a mental hell hole, plagued by my so-called problems. It set me free. I let my list serve as a road map to stay on course—never quitting until my issues were gone. Surprisingly, many issues disappeared quickly. It gave me confidence this was really working. It was like shining a light on bugs at night.

Other issues hung around for a while, but I never lost my commitment to rid myself of them. I was determined to become a new young man, living a life unlike anything I had ever experienced. Doing all this gave me a newfound sense of personal freedom. Best of all, the weight finally lifted off my shoulders. It let me relax—something I had never experienced before.

After a short while, with continued success getting rid of my unwanted issues, I felt a new unconstrained feeling come over me. I no longer felt overwhelmed, angry, sad, or powerless. There was a sweet stillness in this wonderful new void—a feeling of power, joy, and freedom. It spread over my whole life, making living more wonderful. I had no problems. Not one. I smiled because I felt blessed, lucky, free, powerful, and extremely grateful. I finally experienced the Clue Bird's last piece of advice: "and *relax*." I realized the word relax means to be still so you can feel freedom inside of your power.

Turning options into power

As a dad wishing to start fresh with the next generation, I felt compelled to teach my kids how to manage their problems. I bemoaned not having had someone show me the way before Mrs. Wilson taught me what the Clue Bird's message meant. That's why my kids grew up knowing the difference between problems and options. By doing it this way, they sidestepped years of misery and angst. This is the benefit we can give children when we teach them the difference between a real problem and just an option.

Without doubt, kids who master problem management are better Presidents of their *You, Inc.* It gives them a fighting chance and keeps them in control of themselves. Many of us clearly remember how we suffered when we were young. We had to learn how to manage our problems effectively on our own. We survived. We had no other choice. Why risk it with your kids? Commit to showing them the way. If you do, they'll face less pain and suffering, allowing them to move into adulthood with fewer setbacks.

The time kids save by not worrying or fretting about so-called problems can be used on productive endeavors like learning to play an instrument, picking up a hobby like photography, or studying a foreign language. All of this propels them into becoming the victors they were born to be.

We want kids to grow up with a minimum of needless setbacks and troubles. Even when we make it a priority when they're young, they may still experience unnecessary pain and suffering. It's an ongoing process. Children have varying reactions to problems. Fortunately, some kids react very maturely. For these kids, problems are frustrating and time-consuming, but they appear to handle them with little emotion or drama. That's good.

Others, however, become consumed by their problems, and sometimes it affects their physical, mental, and emotional development. This is especially true if they spend an inordinate amount of time worrying, wringing their hands, and fretting over their problems without solving them.

Helping your children become masters of problem management means talking to them about this subject often. Other family members can help too. For example, I taught my children about problems or options, and they taught it to theirs. Yet one night, while visiting with my grandson, I sensed the same sadness and utter feeling of helplessness in him that I had painfully experienced years before. Things were not going well for him. He had buried himself in his so-called problems, feeling out of touch and out of control. Together, we discussed the differences between problems and options.

We talked for a long while about the things I'd learned when my math teacher, Mrs. Wilson, helped me decipher the Clue Bird's message. I could see it helping him, just like it helped me. We weren't just sitting around talking about his mountain of problems—we were looking at options. That's when I knew I'd broken the cycle.

Is it a problem or is it just an option? So, deal with it and relax.

1- Real problems are significant setbacks. Just an option is something unwanted in your life that you can eliminate with your choices.

2- Mislabeling just-an-option as a problem makes everything feel bigger and unsolvable. It needlessly causes angst, feeling over-whelmed, helplessness and makes just-an-op-tion seem like a problem.

3- Real problems are rare. Never fret or worry about so-called problems. Remember, you have a choice in the matter. Pick your best option to eliminate an unwanted issue.

4- Dealing with it means, wholeheartedly committing to implementing the best option from the solutions you identified to solve your unwanted issue until it's gone.

5- Just relax,means being still in the absence of unwanted issues in your life. Feel the freedom you now have because of your power.

Lesson 3

Math

From birth, children have had to acquire new skills on a nonstop basis. Let's face it, we all got on this learning escalator the moment we popped out. Learning anything is difficult. For instance, try learning how to play the piano. I did, and quickly discovered it's frustrating. But learning the piano is optional. Math isn't.

Every schoolchild has to face math. It's not easy at first. To get the right answer, sometimes requires a try-and-fail approach. That's why math teaches children more than just math. It teaches them to deal with the frustration of failure and to keep trying. Good parents help their children master the skills they need to tolerate frustration when they're very young.

Some kids can't do it. That's when math highlights the deficiencies in their mental and emotional growth. It spotlights their shortcomings. If your child is unable to address the frustrations of doing math, the short answer is your child is mentally operating like a much younger child. They are emotionally behind. Monitor your children, watching for signs that they're becoming overwhelmed and uncontrollably frustrated.

With me, I was the perfect student up until about seventh grade. Until then, schoolwork was easy and fun with no homework. The subjects were so basic, I grasped the material intuitively with little effort. However, when seventh grade came, I couldn't adapt to the changes and the new demands of middle school. School abruptly got a lot harder for me.

We were writing themes in English class. There were too many new and difficult subjects to master. It wasn't limited to basic subjects; electives such as music, band, sports, and clubs were now available to us as well. Most of this was new and hard to digest. I felt like I couldn't find enough time to successfully fit it all in. This new, complex mix of activities was overwhelming and frustrating to me. The biggest of all was that algebra suddenly showed its ugly head.

My difficulties lingered way too long because I didn't know what was suddenly wrong with me when I got to seventh grade. I couldn't figure it out. Further adding to this problem was my personal inability to get with it. I honestly didn't want any part of changing gears or getting tough with myself. I liked being a whimsical, carefree kid. Why would I change? My mantra was: it's human nature to resist change.

A few years ago, my grandson was experiencing deep frustration dealing with both his math class and life in general. He isn't alone. I understood that hopeless, miserable feeling all too well because I had the same trouble way back when I was in school.

Back then life was easier, summers were sweeter, and dinosaurs were occasionally seen, according to my children. Regardless, no one prepared me for the type of frustration I was going to face with math or a heavy school load. In school, my frustration slowly built up like a teapot on a stove. Not having the ability to get control, I didn't do well. Every aspect of my life was in shambles.

Academics were terrible. Math class was evil. I was about to get cut from the basketball team for low grades. I even thought some of my friends were making fun of me behind my back. My parents were at their wits' end with me. My siblings made fun of me, causing me to feel like I didn't belong anywhere.

After a very tense meeting with my parents, when they signed my failing report card yet again, I dragged myself to my room to assess my situation. I couldn't figure out why school had suddenly gotten so difficult. I fell asleep totally frustrated but awakened from a dream so real and clear it startled me. Standing in front of me was a beautiful little bird looking directly into my eyes.

He clearly, yet very slowly, said "It's time to make a change. Embrace it and soar." Suddenly awake, I turned on the light. After a while, I sat at my cluttered desk and took out a piece of paper to write down what I had just heard in my dream. I read the message out loud several times, letting the words sink in.

I decided to ask my older brother Dan for help. He was a senior at the time, with everything going his way. He was an honor student, captain of the football, basketball, and baseball teams, president of the student body, and on and on. The next morning, I asked Dan to help me decipher the little bird's statement but skipped the bird part, fearing he would report me as crazy.

Showing him the scribbled statement, I told him about my troubles, admitted how poorly I was doing with everything, and asked for his advice. When Dan agreed to help me, it took me by surprise. Taking the sheet of paper from me, he said we would talk about it later that night.

After dinner, he came into my room and immediately started clearing up my mess to find a place to sit. Feeling uncomfortable, he suggested going to his room. In there, he sternly said he keeps it military clean, out of respect for himself.

With the door shut, we both sat down. Several awkward moments passed without a single word spoken, and then he explained how he had thought about me most of the day. Surprisingly, he said he had been just like me when he was my age.

Deciphering the message

Getting right to it, he said, "The message you gave me means three distinct things." He explained that the first thing was... I had to grow up. It was time for me to make a much-needed mental change. He warned me that it wouldn't be easy. I knew all about what I had to do because he had done it himself. As a freshman in high school, Dan struggled and failed practically everything. He went to his basketball coach for help.

The coach told Dan that he had enough talent to be a star basketball player and could easily play at the college level. According to his coach, Dan's lack of mental and emotional development was setting him back. The coach suggested the way Dan acted like a kid, both on and off the court, proved he was behind in growing up.

His coach said kids who do the bare minimum are fighting to remain kids and don't keep their rooms clean, do chores, schoolwork, or even brush their teeth. He said, "Everything they do is begrudgingly done," and then asked Dan if that sounded familiar. Dan said it was true, and then the coach told him, that if he kept doing the childish, stingy-effort routine he had mastered, he'd become an average adult at best.

Standing up, the coach told Dan it was time to make a change. He told Dan that if he didn't want to change his attitude, he should simply quit the team—so the coach could use that time to develop players who genuinely wanted to improve. After finishing his story, Dan told me he could tell me how to change my life... if I wanted to know.

Embarrassed, I meekly said, "Please help me." Dan said quite sternly, "You dog it by just going through the motions in the classroom, with our family, basketball, and practically everything in your life." He had been brutally honest with me, the way his coach had been with him. It was hard to take. Somehow, inside, I knew it was all true.

According to Dan, as a first step, I needed to drop my minimal-effort approach to life. In its place, he suggested I take on a new hard-work, adult mindset that would put my mind in charge of me instead of my body. Dan explained the best way to do it was to lead myself. He told me to carefully choose and write down my goals. He explained how setting goals would give me something to work on like a possessed person until I achieved them.

The coach had helped Dan set goals for every aspect of his life! Being a member of his family, schoolwork, sports, extracurricular activities, clubs, friends, and community work all fell under this new umbrella of working as if possessed to excel in every aspect of life. He had learned: you must lead yourself to become extraordinary.

My brother moved on to the next part of the Clue Bird message: "Embrace it." He paced his room, saying how it's just words unless you embrace it. It meant I absolutely had to give up acting like a kid because it couldn't work anymore. To make it clear, he explained how it was like trying to wear a favorite sweater you wore in the third grade. It was easy to understand. As much as I might have liked that sweater, it couldn't fit me anymore. I had to discard it. Acting like a kid couldn't work either, so I had to discard it as well.

The third part of the little bird's statement, *and soar*, is a particularly important part of the message. For my brother, it was already happening. He soared. As a freshman, he struggled the way I did in seventh grade. In just three short years, he became living proof that it was time to make a change—time to embrace it and soar. Amazingly, he had successfully adapted a new, focused, hard-working adult attitude.

I wondered why our elders hadn't taught us this very important lesson. It would have saved both of us years of untold suffering and frustration. In their defense, they probably gave us this advice numerous times, but we just didn't hear it. We weren't ready. Sometimes, to really hear something, you have to be ready to receive it. If not, it just goes over your head, like hearing someone speaking in a foreign language. You hear them speaking, but you don't get the message.

Dan also got one more piece of advice from his amazing coach. He told Dan to spread the word by taking the advice he got and to someday pass it on to someone else. Dan continued, "Remember, in life, we get and receive. The very reason we are talking tonight. When you asked me for this advice, just by asking, I knew you were finally ready to hear it."

He told me he had been patiently waiting for this moment, and then he finished by saying he truly loved me as his brother. He fully expected me to outshine him someday. Trying to hide a sly grin, he asked me, as I was leaving his room, if the little bird just happened to be a cardinal. It was!

Applying the message

After my brother enlightened me about the meaning of the Clue Bird's message: "It's time to make a change, embrace it and soar," I started putting my mind in charge of me. I led me. For the first time, I set short and long-term goals. I began making daily "to do" lists to support my goals. This helped me mentally organize every day by simply working from the list of things I'd decided to get done.

Thanks to my brother Dan's advice, I quickly became very efficient in most aspects of my life—just like him. It's proof that what we think about will outwardly become expressed in our lives. That's why we should teach kids how to get their minds right so they can soar.

As I began putting my mind in charge of me, I couldn't help but notice how my little brother was having a struggle of his own. One day, he went to play a game of pickup basketball at an outdoor park. He was terrible. He couldn't get picked for a team, so he just stood there watching. I thought this would be the end of his basketball career. The next day, he spent his allowance money on a basketball and sneakers. He started dribbling in the garage for hours, making life miserable with the incessant banging noise. He lifted weights, then ran ladder and cone drills, which tore up the backyard.

Soon, he was running five miles at a time wearing a weighted backpack. Next, he begged to have a basketball hoop installed in our driveway. He played in the rain and snow. All by himself, beginning with basketball, he had voluntarily changed his mindset from a kid into a new hard-working adult with a vision. He was becoming extraordinary at basketball.

One day, while shooting a game of "out" in the driveway, I couldn't help but ask, "Why do you work at basketball as hard as a college player, but with the rest of your life, you remain very childish and ordinary?" He didn't have a clue.

We discussed how he could become extraordinary in most other aspects of his life if he worked hard at them. After a moment of silence, he looked at me, smiling, and said, "So that's how you and Dan became my heroes?" I told him yes, and we both expected him to do even better.

Everyone wants to maintain the status quo. It's easy. Only do what you want—like playing basketball. Learning how to actually work on frustrating things is something we predictably fight against, causing needless suffering. It's what many children do. Yet Dan changed. He soared.

When he talked to me that night, he had a full schedule. Not only was he captain of three sports teams, he starred in the school play, had community service work, and homework. During our conversation, he asked if I thought he really wanted to go to basketball practice. For him, the answer was, "No, I don't, but yes I do!" He explained how his body says no, but his mind, which is in charge, says yes.

Dan had already been applying the Clue Bird's message. How? He embraced it. And he excelled at everything he did. He made himself extraordinary. My brothers and I were lucky. But without talking to Dan all those years ago, I never would have thought of what he taught me. Never. Just knowing I needed to change my thinking from the viewpoint of a younger child into a new vision of acting like a hard-working adult was a revelation.

The real problem isn't math

Do you remember how you felt growing up? I do. Lots of challenges, tough moments, setbacks, and disappointments. I bet you had them too. That's why we must teach children how to navigate and deal with frustration. The ever-present sense of angst that we all live with never goes away. The thing is... if we don't address how to properly manage frustrations, kids will have to figure it out on their own. Some will sort it out, while others will struggle and fail. Do you want to chance it with your children?

What happens if you don't teach your children how to deal with their frustrations and disappointments? They can develop serious mental and physical problems. Parents can't just decide to leave it alone, hoping their child will somehow figure it out by themselves. Deepening frustration and prolonged failure are serious issues. Failing to make the switch is why we often see twenty-year-old adults acting like they're ten.

Kids must realize having difficulty in school is not a real problem and nothing to be ashamed of. That's why we teach them how to face difficulties, such as math class. We teach them to see it's not the end of the world but just an option or a temporary problem for them to resolve.

It's also a gift, because math class teaches far more than the subject of mathematics. It uncovers the deficiencies in a kid's mental and emotional development. It's a subtle hint that it's time for them to grow up. It means it's time for their parents to help them find another gear. A gear that helps them accept a new, harder-working attitude.

Observe your children, their classmates, or other kids you engage with to notice how they are struggling. It's not math class itself, but what math class is screaming at them. It's screaming that life is getting harder, and everything is not easy. This is something parents can discuss with their children early on so that they will know how to handle the work and deal with the frustration.

Once a parent becomes aware of this issue, they must first guide their child toward managing the frustration by hanging in there until the frustration passes. To do this, we must teach children why trying, failing, and then trying again will work. We must show them how sticking with it gives them the skills to play the piano, write papers, play a sport, or in time, understand math. We must get them to willingly agree to work at it going forward.

Upon reflection, in seventh grade, I had to find a new mental gear to run on. One that allowed me to pay close attention in class. A gear to ask questions when I didn't understand. A gear to finally begin to study and read the material provided. To do *all* the math practice problems for a change.

Further, to start doing *all* of my homework every day, even working ahead to prepare for what was coming. I heard the truth in my brother's words. They instantly made complete sense to me. With this same approach, any child can quickly change their way of doing things. They can learn to tolerate frustration.

More than likely, when prepared to deal with a math-class-type issue, children will know how to work harder to eliminate the problem. Their choice will suddenly make things much easier. Perhaps math class will become enjoyable and no longer a source of frustration. See the problem with math class as a gift.

First, it gives parents the opportunity to help their child grow up, providing an honored chance to work with them to figure out how to do what's needed. Finally, consider that math class, with its difficulties, also shows a child his deficiency. It becomes an opportunity to learn how to work harder with more focus. Mastering frustration not only solves the math class issue but also advances their mental and emotional development.

When raising my kids, I realized how important it was to teach them how to properly address frustration and failure. I proactively addressed this issue on such a repeated basis my kids could never ask me the question, "Why didn't I give them this advice?" They heard it so often, they could teach it. Getting kids to throw away their favorite old sweater and decide to take on a new adult hard-work attitude is critical. It's a part of teaching them to lead themselves by putting their minds in charge instead of their bodies.

That decision alone is transformational. Spare your kids from needless suffering, frustration, or failure. Help them embrace what's coming before the pain sets in. Let's unbridle them of this issue early, letting them get on with becoming the extraordinary victors they were born to become.

**It's time to make a change.
Embrace it and soar.**

1- Math teaches more than math. It highlights deficiencies in mental and emotional growth. Treat learning as a gift because it will wake you up and force you to improve.

2- Put your mind in charge of you and always do what you must first, before doing what you just want to do.

3- Deal with frustration and failure by viewing them as gifts. Frustration and failure is not personal, it's a gift showing you specifically what you need to improve in your journey toward excellence.

4- Become a focused hard worker. Adapt a new mental approach to dealing with frustration and rise to any challenge.

5- Be a rational actor. Live an organized and purpose driven life. Once you identify a deficiency, own it and correct it.

LESSON 4

OWN IT

IT'S HUMAN NATURE to blame unpleasant events on anything besides ourselves. It's easier than owning it. Owning it means having the mindset to take full responsibility for everything in your life, realizing that you created it. Unwanted issues or problems pop up all the time. It's a lifelong dilemma. But if we don't teach this to young kids, they won't admit it when they break a beautiful vase. They might claim they weren't even in the room or even blame a little brother who was asleep at the time.

Children who don't move past blame may later grow up thinking every bad situation is someone else's fault. We don't want kids to grow up this way. That's why teaching kids to own their problems is the critical first step in helping them solve those problems independently, as the president of their *You, Inc.*

Owning it is a mindset that shapes every part of life. For me, it started with baseball. I loved playing. Starting out in little league, I slowly learned the game. I played on several teams, trained with numerous coaches, and felt like I was always making progress. From day one, I was one of the best players.

Middle school came and went. I focused on my quest to become a baseball player, spending hours in batting cages, lifting weights, running sprints, and playing on any team I could. I always felt solid about my growth in the sport. When high school came, I couldn't wait to play baseball at the varsity level. I just knew I was ready for this new chapter in my life. My only concern was my high school had a reputation for being the premier baseball program in town. The talent level on that year's team was outstanding.

During tryouts, I gave it my all and excelled at the drills. Making the varsity squad as a freshman left me beside myself, feeling super proud. I felt like I'd made it. But as the season started, everything changed. Before high school, I had always played short stop. I was a consistent batter, but when the season started that year, I felt remanded to the right field.

Worse, my batting production suddenly hit an all-time low. Putting my head down, I'd slow-walk to the batter's box, chase pitches, and strike out often. I got used to the quick jog back to the dugout, where I'd sit alone on that cold bench after yet another dismal at-bat performance.

Always hard on myself and quick to criticize, I didn't realize my batting performance wasn't that bad for a freshman. I became angry with myself but never admitted it. My frustration and anger got so bad I found myself unable to sleep, constantly worrying. I didn't see any way out of my problem, which left me feeling distraught.

Playing the game with high school seniors who looked like grown men and threw like seasoned pitchers made me look bad at the plate. I stayed upset, overreacting to every setback. I even considered quitting the game altogether. I thought maybe I wasn't really that good after all. Maybe it was just time to move on.

Disturbed from a fitful sleep, I heard the flutter of wings as a little bird landed ever so gently on my shoulder. He whispered, "Becoming extraordinary at anything is entering *rare air*. You can do this. Just get up!" For the next few days, I walked around thinking about his message.

The part about being extraordinary was obvious. I had been working at becoming an extraordinary baseball player my whole life. That's why I instantly understood that every human endeavor is really a pursuit of excellence.

Deciphering the message

Still distraught about my "at bat" problem, I went over to the closed and locked baseball field and climbed the fence. I just needed to be on the field. Slowly, I walked to home plate—an incredibly special place on earth to me. I walked the bases. In my mind, I could hear the cheers from the crowds I'd heard so often. I sat there alone, looking at that empty baseball field. The Clue Bird's advice, "Just get up," hit me like a punch to the gut. What mattered wasn't the problems I faced in my quests for excellence. It was my reactions to those problems.

I started thinking, kids with a dream walk the same difficult trek to excellence—no matter the pursuit. I thought about my situation through the eyes of a chess champion, piano player, doctor, tennis star, all-star golfer, diet center owner, academic scholar, scientist, pilot, and others. I came to understand they all started out as I did. Just like them, I began chasing my dream when I put on my first baseball jersey.

I suddenly believed wholeheartedly that with desire in my heart, I could achieve my dreams. I figured if I wasn't capable of doing something at an excellent level or becoming extraordinary, I wouldn't have had those dreams in the first place.

My reaction to my current dilemma was the only relevant issue at hand. I had to either keep going, struggling even harder, or quit. I had to decide between being a victor or a victim. "Just get up" meant owning my problems. My current problem was caused by me. With the correct response, it would become temporary and easily fixable.

Applying the message

I'm not the only kid who had issues like this. A friend of mine, now a retired NFL player, once told me about his ninth-grade year, when he finally got the chance to play the game he had dreamed about his whole life. Smiling, he said he went to practice loving every minute of it. With laser focus, he spent his weekends working out, determined to get into the best shape of his life. But when the football season finally started, his excitement quickly turned sour because he sat on the bench for almost the entire game.

Even in a 40-0 blowout, he only got in with one minute left. That was all the time he played in that varsity football game. After an emotional pause, he went on with his story, saying, "This still hurts." This last-minute play continued for several games. He just sat there. Each time, the coach motioned him into the game with about a minute left. My friend started thinking he obviously wasn't good enough. Yet somehow, he really didn't believe it.

He blamed the coaches, saying they were just playing their favorites. He suddenly laughed out loud, remembering how, as a sixteen-year-old fourth stringer, he actually thought he knew more about football than the coaches. For a long while, nothing changed.

He finally talked with his dad about his problem, because he started thinking maybe he should just quit the game and move on. During that talk, they both agreed he needed help. They decided he should visit the retired NFL player who just happened to live down the street in his neighborhood.

My friend was super nervous about discussing his problem with a famous world-class athlete. Out of respect, he always addressed him as Mr. Kent. He was relieved to discover he was a surprisingly nice man. After they talked for a while, Mr. Kent told my friend he was too nice to play football. He said he knew this because he had been the same way in high school. He advised my friend to go to church and keep getting good grades. "Why not just do something else?" Mr. Kent asked. But my friend insisted he wanted to keep playing football.

Mr. Kent told him, "Football is a physically tough and demanding game of controlled and planned violence. It's a game you can't play if you're too nice." He added that my friend had an athletic physique that could take him far, but if he wanted to succeed, he had to always practice like he would play. This meant being violent—even in practice with his friends and teammates. Mr. Kent said it would have been easier for my friend to just keep being a nice guy, but he didn't stop there. He also shared how he fixed his nice-guy problem.

He explained that the change had to start with his mindset, with making a deliberate mental shift. What Mr. Kent did was simple but powerful. As soon as he set his foot across the sideline and stepped onto the field, he mentally became the most violent player in the game. Yet off the field, stepping back across the sideline to the bench, he snapped back into his old nice-guy self. My friend, who had also become a retired NFL player, told me doing this fixed his problem. But before he could fix it, he had to own it.

One time, while visiting with my neighbor, out of the blue, he started discussing a problem his daughter was having at school. She had joined the school marching band. She was an outstanding clarinet player who already played in the school's orchestra. However, she also wanted to march in the band. Playing the music was easy for her, but the marching was difficult. Her performance got so bad sometimes, they had to stop practice to work with her personally on the sets and formations.

I was curious about how they solved the problem. As a family, they came up with a host of possible solutions. Their daughter picked the option that made the most sense to her. She decided to fake playing her clarinet, focusing on marching until she got the part down. Slowly, during the formations, she began playing her clarinet more and more. Once she got comfortable playing while marching, her problem vanished. She owned it, and that made all the difference.

The mirror test

Years ago, I had a conversation with a remarkably successful businessman. During our discussion, he took a little coin out of his pocket and handed it to me. It was about the size of a silver dollar. On one side, the coin was smooth, reflecting like a mirror. On the other side was an inscription: "Is that all you got?" I asked the meaning behind the inscription and why he carried the coin.

The businessman told me he used the mirror side to look at himself while saying out loud to the world, "Is that all you got?" Seeing his reflection, he acknowledged that he alone owned his life and everything he possessed. He refused to allow any issue to keep him from attaining his dreams. He vowed to always do the hard work needed to eliminate any problem.

Whenever the businessman defeated an unwanted issue, he held his coin. Grinning, he'd say, "Is that all you got?" Doing this reminded him that the issue had been easy to resolve because he was a victor—never a victim. Successful people owe their whole lives to knowing everything starts and ends with them.

With that in mind, let's end this discussion with your promise to teach your children to just own it by choosing to become the victors they were born to be. Teaching children to own it at a gut level will prepare them to find solutions to rid themselves of the problems they create.

We want children to look at the person in the mirror as the place to blame their troubles. When children can't do this, they avoid owning their problems in one of three ways. First, they might become masters at the blame game. They deflect ownership of their problems onto something else—anything else.

In their minds, it has nothing to do with them because they always view themselves as perfect, or flawless. They become know-it-alls. They're the ones who say it's not their fault when they fail their English class. They blame the failing grade on the terrible teacher. They squawk, claiming she's mean, nobody likes her, and many are failing her miserable class.

A second way to avoid owning it is to ignore it. Some children act as though the unwanted issue doesn't exist. They try to work around the issue as long as they can, never addressing or fixing anything. The third way to avoid owning it is to quit. These kids get angry and frustrated, and in an irrational moment, they quit—quit school, quit jobs, quit anything related to their problem. Soon after, they find out quitting doesn't fix anything. It only adds to the problem.

Teach your child to embrace their problems without getting embarrassed by having even a single moment with an issue. A batting slump, three-putts, missing free throws, or failing at school are not really problems. They're life issues that tell your child where to focus. They show them where they're lagging behind and uncover their need to work harder in their journeys to excellence.

After choosing an option with your child, help them work hard every day to implement their chosen solution, like a possessed person. Make sure they don't quit until they're finally free of their unpleasant issue. I know this works because by owning it, I made short order of fixing my batting problem.

I chose to stay positive, work harder with the bat, and take extra hitting practice every day. I stayed positive, believing the extra work would pay off by improving my hitting statistics. I stuck to it like a possessed person. It worked.

Eliminating problems with focused hard work can help a child suddenly become a better player, student, or both. Teach them to always see a problem as just something to work on or improve while actively avoiding emotionally charged thoughts. That kind of nonsense only makes it harder to solve or eliminate problems. Teach them not to let their emotions get in the way or create new problems. Teach them to quickly fix their problems using a chosen option, then use focused hard work to rid themselves of the problem for good.

Every child can experience what the Clue Bird advised: "Becoming extraordinary at anything is entering rare air." They just need to get up and do it. They can become their dreams. In some ways, problems are gifts showing us our shortcomings. Getting up is owning, selecting, and implementing your best option to eliminate your problem. It's not lying down, whining, and wanting to quit.

Becoming extraordinary at anything is entering rare air. You can do this, just get up.

1- You can become extraordinary, entering rare air. Your reaction to your problems matters more than the problem itself.

2- In your steep, climb to excellence you will face numerous setbacks or problems along the way. Own it. They are gifts.

3- Avoid the blame game or self-doubt. If you quit an endeavor you'll never master it. You must own it to fix and eliminate your problems.

4- Own your whole life and not just your problems. The mirror is the first place to look to find who is responsible for your troubles.

5- As the president of your *You, Inc.* learn to solve your problems independently. Adapt a mindset that says, own everything in your life, by realizing you created it.

Lesson 5

Know it all

I'VE BEEN SUBJECTED to many know-it-all types of people. They're everywhere. I've experienced them as preteens, teenagers, middle-aged and retirees. They come from all ages, sexes, and walks of life. It's easy to recognize a know-it-all. A know-it-all will take over every conversation or explain every aspect of any subject, right or wrong, leaving practically no room for anyone to speak.

They talk down to their siblings, considering them uninformed as they lecture them on a practically nonstop basis. In peer settings, they dominate their friends and offer unwelcomed, offhand solutions to practically any problem. If you observe any of this behavior with your kids, correct it quickly and at home.

I think these people who seem to know it all can be young or old, male or female, and come from diverse backgrounds. They take their audience hostage while injecting their perceived wisdom into every conversation. Friends, relatives, strangers—no one is spared. They're like the guy in the room with his zipper down. They're the only one who doesn't know how annoying they are. Who would ever risk confronting them? It's not worth it. They're oblivious. I'm betting this habit starts in childhood and just keeps growing.

The other night, I attended a casual dinner with my grandson and several of his friends. It quickly became obvious that one of his friends thoroughly dominated the conversation. He not only talked the most, but he also had a know-it-all attitude. His behavior was annoying.

I could tell by the looks in my grandson's friends' eyes and their body language that they were very annoyed with him. I wasn't surprised that my grandson and his close-knit group of friends hadn't confronted their know-it-all friend about his behavior. It may not have mattered if they did.

For example, my stepfather was a brilliant man. He wore us out letting us know just how smart he was by spending hours educating us about everything, whether he understood it or not. Confronting him didn't change anything. He just kept talking until we either fell asleep or left the room. I think younger know-it-alls are more malleable. When they finally become aware of their obnoxious behavior, they quickly change.

In high school, I had a friend named Harold. I'll never forget him because he was a classic know-it-all, and I was probably his only friend. Day after day, it was the same. He'd take over conversations, spewing his unwanted superior knowledge. It didn't matter if we were joking around or working on a class project—Harold always went into know-it-all mode.

Later, when we were alone, I'd try to talk to him about it. I'd tell him he came off as condescending, that he never let anyone else get a word in, and that his behavior was offensive. He'd slump his head, wring his hands, and say he was sorry. He'd promise to change, saying he'd never do it again. But the next time it happened, I'd have the same conversation with him, searching for the right words to make him see his problem and finally own it.

In my discussions with Harold, I shared what I'd learned about fixing problems. I was trying to get him to become aware of his offensive behavior so he could own it. Frustratingly, I was getting nowhere. I gave him every piece of advice I could think of to help him identify, own, and pick an option to eliminate his know-it-all problem. It seemed hopeless. Unable to bear his unpleasant behavior for one more day, I considered dropping him as a friend.

I was ready to give up on him. But that night, as if by magic, a beautiful little Clue Bird appeared in my dream. He landed gently on my shoulder and whispered, "Listen to the world, and then respond." The dream was so real, it jolted me awake. I lay there in the dark, wrestling with the message, unable to fall back asleep.

Deciphering the message

Aggravated, I got up. Sitting in my room, I thought about that message. What did it mean? First, I wondered if this was about how to help Harold or something else entirely. It was getting light outside before it dawned on me this message was for anyone, but it was also perfect for Harold. I quickly broke down what the Clue Bird said on a sheet of paper. The first part, "Listen to the world first," was a gotcha moment for me. It reminded me of my grandmother, who didn't have a formal education due to her circumstances growing up. Yet, she was one of the wisest human beings I ever knew.

One day when I was acting like a brat, being loud, obnoxious, and talking too much, my grandmother pulled me aside. Pointing her index finger at me while rapidly moving it up and down, remarkably close to my face, was a sure sign of my imminent personal danger. Looking me in the eye, she said, "You have two ears and only one mouth for a good reason." I understood.

She wanted me to listen twice as much as I talked. Remembering it, I thought maybe it was the best piece of advice I ever got. I could see how, by listening we find out exactly what someone is thinking. We're able to shape our response more accurately to complement the conversation. For example, at school or work, when someone gets up to talk about the subject at hand, careful listening helps us ascertain what the speaker knows about the topic.

Thinking about what my dear grandmother told me years before, I came to see how we might use our two ears twice as much as our mouth. It seemed two to one was the correct ratio between listening and speaking. Maybe heeding the advice to "listen to the world first" would make me a truly great listener and help me fully comprehend what someone else says. But the second part—*and then respond*—seemed harder.

The listening part is passive. You just sit there, doing nothing, while listening and digesting what someone is saying to you. Responding is the active part. It means responding to what you heard after careful consideration. I figured it was difficult because a response can either bless or damn you, and everything in between.

I realized with all the coaching and counseling I had laid on my friend, I had never addressed with Harold what the Clue Bird just told me. That was to listen. This was the missing piece. It was good advice for me too. My whole approach with Harold had been about getting him to talk less, be quiet, or simply shut up. To stop dominating conversations, and to stop trying to enlighten everyone with his wisdom. But I had never thought to say, "just listen." I could hardly wait to tell him and see what happened.

Applying the message

My talk with Harold started with getting him to admit he came off as a know-it-all. We spent at least an hour going through his alibis. He said he got nervous when people didn't talk, insisted his friends really didn't know as much as he did, and claimed he was doing them a favor by educating them. On and on it went. After explaining how annoying those things were, I finally dragged it out of him to own it. He admitted he was responsible for this issue—and no one else. He had taken the first step needed to change his behavior.

Immediately, we discussed his options. I finally injected what the Clue Bird had told me. I shared how he might "listen to the world first and then respond." The first test came after we'd rehearsed this new and exciting approach a few times. We were in the physics lab, and the teacher assigned a group of us to complete a lab experiment. First, we needed to discuss the project as a group and then distribute the experiment tasks amongst the group.

Harold planned to study physics in college, so he typically took over these types of projects in full know-it-all mode. Without thinking, he would assign most of the important stuff to himself, leaving everyone else out of the decisions and assignments. After that, he might set up due dates for the various parts of the project, all the way up to its final presentation. It was always a disaster, with everyone having a terrible attitude about both know-it-all Harold and his lousy project.

Not this time. To my amazement, to start off our meeting, he simply looked around and calmly said to the group, "Tell me how everyone wants to do this project. I'll just take notes and shut up." I could hear my heartbeat. It was so quiet in the lab that day. Slowly, at first, one by one, we started talking, fully expecting him to interrupt us. I'm sure we were waiting for Harold to snap back into his old self, but to his credit, he didn't.

There are always classmates or coworkers like Harold walking around. With a little coaching from someone or a group, they might go from being a know-it-all who dominates every conversation to just a regular person. The Clue Bird advice worked. Harold followed this advice from then on.

My backroom coaching of Harold was akin to preparing a prize-fighter for a ten-round bout. It got him warmed up and ready for the task at hand. Eventually, he made new friends, got invited to outings and parties, and then went off to college a new man.

The power of listening first

To teach children to become real listeners, they need to focus completely on what others are saying, without the distraction of their own thoughts. Too often, people are so busy preparing what they're going to say that they miss much of what's actually being said. To reinforce this with my kids, I read them stories and quizzed them on the details, offering small prizes for correct answers. Listening to win made them excellent listeners.

At times, allow others to keep talking. Don't let them off the hook by speaking up or asking a question. Just let them keep going. You'll be surprised by what you learn. You'll then know how to respond more accurately when they finally stop. This is fully in alignment with what the Clue Bird told me years ago: "Listen to the world."

I taught my children to match a speaker's words with their nonverbal cues so they could understand the full message. This aligned with advice my grandmother gave me years ago. I reminded my kids that they only have one mouth and should use it sparingly and wisely, always keeping some concern for what they say. The good thing is that true listening often means you don't have to say much at all. I wish I'd learned that lesson earlier in life.

Let's start early and teach our kids how to really listen, so they don't have to learn it the hard way or risk becoming know-it-alls who never listen. It takes practice, but children can learn to think before they speak. In conversations, they must always be careful about what's said because words can't ever be taken back.

If we teach kids to listen more than they talk, they'll likely never develop a know-it-all problem like my old friend Harold. At home, we can gently and privately address this behavior, offering options for change before it becomes a bigger issue. If left uncorrected, these kids may face harsh lessons outside the home—being called out, ignored, or even hazed by their peers.

Know-it-alls have always existed, and they're likely to be around eons from now. It's better to catch this habit early because you don't want your kid going around dominating conversations, correcting others, or making every interaction about their own knowledge. We all have to put up with this problem from classmates, relatives, and coworkers, but let's spare our kids.

Further, kids should think of their mouths as the gas pedal on their car. Their mouths will move them through life because of what they say. Unlike a thought, once you say something and others hear, see, or read it, it's no longer just yours. So go through life thinking about anything you want, but speak carefully. It's a great time for kids to realize just how powerful their words can be. They should learn that their spoken words can carry them to heights they never dreamed of.

An additional point to consider is this: unlike during my school days, when we communicated with smoke signals, we now live in a digital age. For the first time in history, most of us possess a digital mouth. It's just like your biological mouth. You can use it to become a virtual know-it-all. This kind of know-it-all can be worse, and it's just as important for kids to control their electronic mouth.

I taught my kids to always remember, before they hit the send button, to think about whether what they intend to send could stand the scrutiny of being posted as a headline in the local newspaper. They should be careful with social media, texting, email, and the internet. I told them if not—don't send it. Kids should understand that what's out there may seem fine while they're in school, but someday, it might cost them a job.

Another way to think of this is that if we learn to carefully listen and monitor what we say, we can avoid being disappointed in ourselves. We might consider ourselves better human beings than what's coming out of our mouths.

To summarize, after all our discussion about the various people in our lives, with particular attention to the know-it-all types, remember the Clue Bird's advice: "First listen to the world, and then respond." Let's teach kids to become great listeners—not just to hear others, but to really listen. Next, they need to learn how to carefully measure their responses, either verbally or electronically, always seeking to be the gift in the room.

Listen to the world first and then respond.

1- Know-it-alls come in all ages, educational levels, sexes, and often exhibit condescending, rude and obnoxious behavior.

2- Great listeners focus on what is being presented doing nothing else. Remember, to listen twice as much as you speak, as you have two ears and one mouth.

3- Thoughts are your private domain, your secrets and sole possessions, but what you speak, write or send out into the world, belongs to the world. This can be either a blessing, damnation or anything in between.

4- Your mouth runs your life. Remember, words can't ever be taken back. The spoken word is powerful and can determine your future, both good and bad.

5- Words are thoughts converted into action, revealing what you are made of. Listen to what you say and correct any deficiencies on your journey to excellence.

LESSON 6

HARD WORK ATTITUDE

PARENTS DON'T EXPECT much from infants; our focus is growing them up and keeping them healthy. With preteens, we start asking them to do things for themselves. They're assigned household chores, often met with stiff resistance because they want to keep being little kids—having their parents continue doing everything for them. With constant coaching, we get them to reluctantly do basic chores. Even then, our requests are often met with constant complaining, delays, and poor performance.

Later, as teens, we ask them take on even more household chores. Schoolwork and sports also add to what's required of them. Still, the constant drumbeat we hear is their reluctance to grow up. The whining, complaining, and poor performance can be frustrating. They fight to keep being kids coddled by their parents. The underlying goal is helping kids give up their minimal-effort attitude and embrace a much-needed new hard-work attitude.

Years ago, when I talked with my daughter about her upcoming volleyball season, I thought she would be excited. As a senior, it was her last year—but she lamented that the game wasn't exciting to her anymore. She felt volleyball was a waste of time. I advised her to *be* a volleyball player. I suggested she take note of her teammates and pick out the practice players.

Those were the players whose biggest asset was just being handy to have around in case of an injury. My questions for her were: Are you one of the excellent players who live and breathe volleyball? Are you willing to do whatever it takes to get better and better?

Our conversation got me thinking about my high school days playing sports—way back when they had just dug the Erie Canal. I showed up to practices with little interest or effort and sadly watched most of our games from the bench. I was quick to complain about how the coaches always played their favorites. My response was typical for a high school athlete. I was probably right about the coaches always playing their favorite players. But not for the reasons I selfishly settled on.

I thought about how miserable I felt back in school. So miserable that one afternoon, I examined every crevice of my life. On a piece of paper, I labeled one side the good side and wrote down everything I did in an excellent manner.

On the other side, the bad side, I wrote down everything I performed at an average level—or maybe even a little mediocre. Soon enough, I realized I wasn't excellent at anything. In anger, I tore the paper into shreds. I concluded I was mediocre at best and it was all my fault. I had gotten lazy.

Yet I was surrounded every day by classmates who were excellent at many things. In my moment of self-pity, asking why, I had no excuse. I had the benefit of great family and friends. I was smart and athletic too. So, it begged the question: What's the matter with me? I asked it repeatedly. Nearly in a frenzy, I paced my room, feeling thoroughly disgusted with myself. Immersed in self-loathing, I finally went to bed.

In my dream, a beautiful little bird stood on my shoulder. Curiously, all he said was, "Be a hard worker and enjoy your achievements." No longer tired, I turned on every light in my room, got dressed, and then sat at my desk. I thought about what the little clue bird had said. I also wondered what it might mean and whether his advice could help me.

Deciphering the message

I wrote down what the Clue Bird said, deciding to make sense of it and improve my miserable life. *Be a hard worker and enjoy your achievements* seemed simple enough. Just reading it, I had to agree with the little bird's message. My first question was: Why did he say, "Be a hard worker," and not just, "Do a good job"? That required a little exploration on my part.

Two distinct events challenged my minimal-effort thinking back then. The first happened one afternoon when several of us went down to the ball field to toss frisbees. Two of our teammates were already there, but they weren't tossing frisbees. They were running hundred-yard sprints at a jailbreak pace—one after another. I lost count at twenty-two. I wondered why they were running sprints. The answer quietly came to me. They were only freshmen, but also starting outfielders on our team.

The second instance happened at a teammate's house, where I went to get a little help with my English homework. While walking through his garage, I noticed a batting tee, about ten baseball bats, batting gloves, and two large pails of baseballs under a large net.

When I asked about them, he said that after doing his homework and cleaning his room—but before taking a shower—he hit three hundred balls off the batting tee into the net. *Wow*, I thought, suddenly realizing his extra effort was why he won honors for his batting average every year. He also made All-State and hoped to play baseball in college.

Reflecting on their hard work answered my question. It was about who they were being. These players were rising stars. It came to me that there is a vast difference between being something and doing something. Doing something sounds like a job.

For example, I figured if I got hired to spread a truckload of gravel in the hot sun with a shovel and needed to have it done by nightfall, it would seem like a terrible job. I might do it—or try to do it—but it would feel like a chore, or an awful job. My heart wouldn't be in it. I wasn't born to shovel gravel, I would whine.

This all applied to me. How would shoveling gravel be any different from how I played baseball? I had only been doing baseball all along. I wasn't a baseball player. I showed no effort in practice, just lifelessly going through batting practice. I often checked my watch during practice because I was tired and couldn't wait for it to end, feeling like I had more important things to do.

Putting on the uniform didn't make me a baseball player. I faked it. My heart wasn't in it. I didn't own it. I didn't do whatever it took to become better. Baseball wasn't a job—it was a labor of love. During my senior year, my attitude of just doing things held me back. Being something was what I lacked in schoolwork, in sports, in friendships, and in practically every aspect of my life. I missed out. It made me mediocre.

The Clue Bird was right. I had to be a hard worker. That was the key difference between doers who treat life like a job and do the minimum, and the ones who are being. Being means doing whatever it takes—becoming an even a better version of yourself through boundless hard work.

Applying the message

What was the difference between the two freshmen who were running sprints and me? The answer is simple: they were baseball players. They were doing extra work outside of normal practice to get even better. As outfielders, they knew speed was their friend when running down fly balls. They were out there hustling, doing sprint work to improve their play. Other teammates, like me, relaxed by tossing a frisbee and got nothing done to improve our game.

It's the core difference between being something and just doing something. Being something means your actions come from the heart, while doing something is akin to a job. Being is who you are down to your soul. You'll do whatever it takes to keep being—a baseball player, a surgeon, a pianist—whatever is in your heart. The person just doing-something is a fraud. Everything is an obligation. They do the minimum.

Let's look at firefighters. To select only fitting candidates, they weed out applicants, focusing on academics, interviews, physical exams, and fitness testing. It's a lengthy and necessary process. Even after being selected, applicants must pass the required training to earn their badge. It takes hard work.

Finally, they become a newly minted firefighter, proudly assigned to a firehouse as its newest asset. After all that effort, I'd bet there are few, if any, new firefighters who are just whimsically doing the job. That's not possible because they wouldn't have been hired in the first place. They wouldn't have finished the training.

Besides, with a doing attitude, they'd treat it like a job—doing the minimum to just get by. Is there anyone among us who would want to run into a burning building with a fellow firefighter who is just doing his job? Just doing the minimum? Of course not. You can't do firefighter. You have to be a firefighter. Being a firefighter means being the absolute best at what they do. It's a pride thing. Many in this field work hard to be their best, if for no other reason than knowing their fellow firefighters can rely on them when in peril.

In college, I got that deep-down sense of knowing what it meant to be something instead of just doing something. One day, I visited an air show with my friends. Part of the experience was sitting in the cockpit of a fighter jet. With a little coaxing, I got all my friends to wait in the long line. I put up with their complaining until we started up the ladder to sit in that beautiful aircraft. With assistance, I was right there, experiencing it.

For a couple of minutes, I sat there, motionless. I didn't hear a word the display pilot said to me. In that surreal moment, the pulse shooting through my body foreshadowed what I'd be someday—without a doubt. Right then, I mentally became a pilot. Buoyed by the dream in my heart, I worked like a possessed person to achieve it. My new hard-work attitude drove me to excellence in my physical training and schoolwork. The sudden change was so dramatic that my friends kept asking what happened to me.

Things really did change. But it never really felt like hard work, because from that day forward, it was simply a labor of love—working to become what I already envisioned in my imagination.

Being takes hard work

Some kids spend more time trying to get out of things than it would take to just voluntarily do them. I constantly told my kids, "If you had just done the chore you're complaining about in the first place, it would be done by now." That applied to schoolwork, sports, chores, and personal hygiene.

I was often puzzled about how to help them grow up mentally and emotionally to acquire that much-needed hard work attitude. At some point, every child has to adopt a hard-work attitude in order to become successful. We just can't accurately predict how or when.

Scrutinize your kids to determine which group they're in. No matter what the activity—schoolwork, sports, theater—take a serious look.

Are they just doing something, or are they, in their hearts, being something? You'll know. Talk to them. Use their sports team, their role in a play, or whatever they're doing in their lives to start the conversation. Sit down together. Listen, and then respond. Ask if your points hit home. Can they pick out the kids who are just doing it? Can they see and feel the difference?

You can see when kids shift to a grown-up way of thinking. These kids might get up early to run five miles before school, stay after practice to hit an additional hundred volleyball serves, or do survival workout sessions with a professional strength trainer. If so, the kid is being in life.

Their hard-work ethic likely rubs off on their academics. I'll bet they're a good and dependable friend. Kids like these keep their rooms clean and rarely get in trouble. Everything they do is at an excellent level because their hard work ethic is a big part of being all those things.

In contrast, kids who are *just doers* have a far different story. They'll be average in school, average in sports, and average in just about everything. They put in only the minimal effort needed to get things done. In all responsibilities, they seek to just get by, often making them mediocre. As doers, they treat every aspect of their lives like a job. Life, for them, is very much like having a job they don't want.

As they say, "The harder you work, the luckier you get." And it's true. You simply can't fake hard work. Working hard is the bedrock of success, and children must learn this. The signs that show a child is still a doer, someone who puts in minimal effort, shows up in their actions.

If you were to honestly describe your child, what would you say? If you asked your kids to describe themselves, or asked a sibling about another sibling, what would they say? The answers to these questions will tell you whether your child has a hard work attitude.

When I reflected on my senior year, I realized varsity sports had become something I'd just gotten used to. The excitement was gone. Playing had somehow lost its luster. As an older person who played baseball with wooden bats and pine tar, my senior year should've been about being "our last year" and "going out with a bang" kind of bravado.

Strangely, I was thinking just the opposite. I just wanted to get through it—to move on. Looking back helped me understand why my daughter felt the way she did. But our talk about being versus doing helped her stay on track.

Just like my daughter, your child can learn the difference too. Being something changes how you show up. Doers aren't the *first in line* for practice drills, they mostly hang at the back, watching the starters work through their drills with maximum effort.

Then, the doers nervously slide through, just trying to get by, giving the coaches no confidence that they're ready or willing to perform in a varsity match. In practice scrimmages, doers play with a little hesitation. They're never the ones who want the ball with the game on the line. It's a lack of work ethic. Have a talk with your kids, and they'll never be this way.

Start your child out right by helping them adopt a hard-work attitude early. Doing so will guide them to become something of their own choosing. Then all their labors, setbacks, heartaches, and frustrations won't matter, because their efforts will be a labor of love—leading them to fulfill a purpose they once only imagined. Dreams make becoming a hard worker easy. When kids live this way, they can enjoy all their achievements, just like the Clue Bird said.

Be a hard worker and enjoy your achievements.

1- There is a vast difference between being something and doing something. Being something is a labor of love, while just doing something is like having a job you must do and don't want.

2- Being something is soul deep. It means, your maximum effort comes from your heart. In stark contrast, to just do something is like doing a job.

3- A hard-work attitude spews a sense of being or becoming, that effortlessly transforms into a hard work ethic.

4- Fall in love with something. The effort spent on what you love will no longer feel like work, as it becomes a pleasure and a labor of love.

5- It's satisfying becoming something by working hard at what you chose, so enjoy your achievements as you've earned them.

Lesson 7

Living Ahead of Yourself

OUR KIDS HAD NO idea who they were when they came into this wonderful world. Only being mattered, not where they were, or why they were here. What's more, at birth, they were completely dependent on the adults in their lives. They were completely helpless, yet somehow survived. Kids learn to adapt to many things—everything, really. Physically, they learn to brush their teeth, bathe, and dress themselves. A little later, they learn how to play sports and maybe ride a bike.

Socially, they learn how to get along with others, behave in public, and make and keep friends. They also learn how to behave at home and in school. Mentally, their growth is impressive. Eventually, they learn to talk, express themselves, make friends, and complete their schoolwork simultaneously. And that's what makes living ahead possible.

Living ahead requires planning and execution. Why? Because it's easy to live behind yourself, as looking back gives you twenty-twenty vision. A parent's job is to teach their kids to mentally live proactively and to remain ahead of themselves by planning their lives. Children must understand that planning involves imagining a future and then deciding how to get there. It's the way to plan ahead. Doing this means children are mentally living in their futures and figuring out how to look ahead.

We all remember how hard life can feel when we're young. Ask any middle school kid if they think being in third grade again would be a piece of cake—I bet they do. Why? Because kids often think where they are now is exceedingly difficult, simply because they live reactively in the present. When they reach middle school, the regular dynamics of growing up change. It's a period when learning new things makes that leg of their journey even more challenging.

Beginning in middle school, learning demands are mixed with foreign languages, sports, music, theater, and even more chores at home. This big change requires planning and organizational skills. What makes this period increasingly difficult is the demand that children match their mental and emotional growth with their physical growth. At this juncture, kids need to mentally live ahead of themselves.

Living ahead means becoming organized. It means helping kids live proactively. As life gets more complex, they no longer have the luxury of reacting by whimsically doing whatever they choose whenever they feel like it. Being late, disorganized, and forgetful are habits that describe their behavior until they learn to do better. We must replace those habits with new ones, such as being organized, planning, and living ahead.

Living reactively is mostly how kids cope. During a recent visit with my grandson, we talked about his frustrations. He felt bogged down by the new, never-ending demands of sports, schoolwork, friends, and family. He felt like he was climbing a steep hill, losing energy, and dreading he wouldn't make the cut.

He had little free time. "I can't seem to catch my breath," he confessed. "Life feels overwhelming, depressing, and sad. Life shouldn't feel like this. How do I get out of this jail?" he moaned. I told him I had once felt the same way. I said his predicament was quite common and that practically every young adult feels the way he does at some point.

My grandson, like many, incorrectly concluded that something must be wrong with him, thinking he didn't measure up. He felt somewhat depressed; his life was no longer fun, and he felt it had become too mixed up, busy, and complicated. His despair came from not knowing how to fix things. At his age, my deepest frustration about life was feeling out of control. I was behind in school, working as hard as I could, but couldn't fix anything. I felt hopeless.

One strange night, the Clue Bird magically landed on my shoulder. In my dream, he whispered in my ear, "Don't get frustrated, get organized. Plan your life." I woke up and couldn't get his words out of my mind. After failing to go back to sleep, I finally got up. While finishing a half-eaten candy bar I found under my bed, I pondered what the message meant.

Finally, I wrote it down so I wouldn't forget, because somehow, deep down, I knew it was extremely useful advice. I wondered if the Clue Bird's message could be the key to fixing the disorder in my life.

Deciphering the message

At daybreak, it dawned on me that my life had gotten so busy, my no-plan, whimsical approach to life—which I had successfully run on up until then—wasn't working anymore. Life seemed to be an ever-accelerating event. It came at me fast and hard. This mattered because I wanted to figure out how to adapt to the increasing velocity.

Lacking a plan, I was only reacting to the events popping up in my life. I was doing things with maximum effort, staying busy like a buzz-saw, haphazardly trying to do everything I needed to get done. Like a spinning top burning lots of energy, I made little progress because my efforts were unfocused.

Living like that made me miserable and frustrated. I started to hate my life. Sound familiar? Responding to the Clue Bird's message meant I had to make changes. I knew I would experience a miserable, frustrating life until I somehow learned to plan. I didn't really know where to start, but I took out a pencil and paper.

I tried to look at the big overview of everything that was coming. It got me thinking about life from the perspective of a three-year-old. They didn't really have anything to do, but life for them could be frustrating, ever-changing, and full of things they needed to do anyway—even if it only meant torturing the dog, deciding what to play with (like a misplaced fork they happened upon), or eating a banana they found in the couch. Life seemed hard, difficult, and confusing for them.

My teenage life was obviously more physically and mentally advanced than that of a three-year-old. Being older, I realized I needed to do planned things every day, because with each passing year, the number of things I had to accomplish continued to grow. To do what the little bird said, I had to be more mature.

As teenagers are obviously far more physically and mentally advanced, developed, and mature than they were at three, I figured my to-do lists had become vastly different as well. To get started, I tried to plan each month by writing down the things I might find on a typical to-do list:

- ✓ Study for the Spanish quiz on the ride to school
- ✓ Work in study hall for the math test
- ✓ Get the questions about my book report answered
- ✓ Basketball practice today after school
- ✓ Strength and conditioning today
- ✓ Several guys told me to talk to Coach about another position
- ✓ Complete the book report that's due tomorrow
- ✓ Math & History homework

It seemed to me that if I could execute my daily to-do plans, it would allow me to achieve those desired outcomes. I kept thinking this might make my life more predictable, much easier, and more enjoyable. For example, if I planned to earn an "A" in math class the next grading period, I would need to do my math lessons every day and make sure it was on my to-do list. I was certain that if I completely studied my math lessons and did all the homework—no surprise—I'd earn an "A" as planned.

Applying the message

Teachers are masters at using a syllabus. Back when I studied by candlelight, I was always handed a syllabus on the first day of class. It listed the first and last day of school, included the dates of the holidays, teacher planning days, midterms, quizzes, the final exam, and additional due dates for book reports or special projects. With it, I could have planned what I needed to do. But you probably guessed it—I didn't. What did I do? I tossed them. Yes, I thought they were unimportant. I was too busy *not* having time to read it, and I never used them.

Remembering the Clue Bird's message: "Don't get frustrated, get organized. Plan your life." I started using those syllabuses. Planning provided order and reduced my frustration. I committed to planning out the remainder of the year in a syllabus format. For every upcoming month, I included everything I thought might happen: birthdays, holidays, vacations, school days, sports schedules, and more. Each month got filled with as much additional detail as possible. I learned to treat my plan like a living document. My newly created personal syllabus became my roadmap. It made filling in each week in advance much easier. Doing things this way, I could change it as often as needed. It became my *see-over-the-horizon* document.

Eight to five is prime time. It's the peak productive period for mental and physical abilities. That's why I acknowledged how time thieves could subtly ruin my daily plans. It became important for me to jealously guard against them, especially in prime time. I needed to set limits. Prime time had to be about the business at hand. Time thieves needed to be politely put off until later. I learned to guard my prime time with laser-like focus, getting my daily to-do lists done as early as possible each day to avoid falling further and further behind, adding to my frustration.

To jealously guard my prime time, all my socializing had to wait until evening. I thought about a fighter pilot zipping along just above the trees during the prime time of his day. Would he be concurrently prioritizing his to-do list? No—he'd steadfastly remain alert and focused, ignoring all else, performing the dangerous job at hand. I had to do the same.

In eighteen short years, kids grow from infants into young adults. Parents know growing up is frustrating. We've all watched kids struggle to learn new things—playing soccer or speaking a second language comes to mind. Those eighteen years go fast and mark the leg of the journey where children are challenged to keep learning more and more complex things. As a dad, I brought what I learned from the Clue Bird to my kids. Early on, I showed them how to plan to live ahead of themselves.

Referring to their syllabuses, show your kids how to complete their daily to-do lists at least the night before—if not sooner. With my children, initially and for a while, we wrote them out together, doing several days at a time. Likewise, for a time, check both their syllabus and their to-do lists to continue teaching them how to plan. Teaching this is how they will finally eliminate much of the frustration and suffering they might feel when trying to get things done. It's their payoff.

Some kids won't get the Clue Bird's message, and they won't change. They'll continue acting whimsically, directionless, and haphazardly. Like a spinning wheel on ice, they'll get nowhere. Lacking a plan, they only react to the events popping up in their lives. They'll just keep falling further behind while working hard, because their efforts will be unfocused. You do not want this to happen to your children.

Hindsight is not planning

Very early on, kids should learn that planning is *the key* to getting important things done and living a balanced, joyful life. Have them think of a wild animal in the wilderness. They don't live by the law of minimal effort; they do whatever's needed to stay alive, eat, reproduce, and survive to fight another day. They don't plan or start each day with a vision of how they'll grow or flourish.

They simply react to whatever they face—it's moment by moment. Every day is about survival. Nothing more. Upon awakening, it's *fights on*: finding food, water, and fending off predators. At the start, they're charged up, fully alert, but as the day wears on, they tire, making them more vulnerable. It's always survival mode.

It makes me glad I'm not a bobcat, having to hunt for survival. Thankfully, kids don't have to live by the law of survival. They're human beings—smart, walk erect, equipped with opposable thumbs, imagination, and a drive to succeed. Unlike wild animals, they can plan for tomorrow and shape their future. That's why teaching them to plan is giving them the tools to do more than just survive by the laws of minimal effort—it's about helping them thrive.

Let's represent the waning usefulness of a day as an hourglass. We all get the same amount of sand in our hourglass each day. At the start, the hourglass is full of sand, making us ready for anything. As the day goes on, the sand streams through the narrow opening, never stopping. Sand drains from the upper bulb and we lose energy. Even though we wake up refreshed with an hourglass full of sand, by dinnertime our minds and bodies are drained from the stress of the day.

From dinner until bedtime, kids are not nearly as alert and "with it" as they think they are. Their bodies are winding down, preparing for their much-needed rest—right when they're tasked with doing their homework. They may also need to take out the trash, do the dishes, tend to the dog, and tackle whatever other real-life issues come up. This is hard on them. As we know, the plan to do homework after dinner often blows up. Homework doesn't get done. Again.

While your child considers what to put on their to-do list, guide them with the wild animal example. Remind them that when they wake up each morning, they are fresh, wide awake, and ready. It becomes *fights on* time. Each day, they should include everything they need to do, followed by what they want to do—time permitting. Make sure they start with the hardest or most disagreeable things first, working down to the easier ones.

Have them write it on a three-by-five card or a sheet of paper. Some might use a computer or phone. Essentially, it's not important how they keep track, but they should carry their to-do list around and check off items as they complete them. What's important, however, is that they do this every day, giving them a daily roadmap. Using their to-do lists, my kids often bragged about all they had accomplished. They enjoyed making progress as they checked off each item throughout the day.

With their roadmap in hand, help them jealously guard against time thieves—especially in prime time. Ensuring they limit TV, phone, computer, email, and social media use is a way to help them get back countless lost minutes each day. Most of it is wasted time anyway. It's addictive. The proof? Even though they shouldn't be on social media during prime time, they still do it. Their alibi: "Everyone is trading messages and checking what someone posted." This kind of electronic social activity is needless and not a productive use of their time.

If warranted, parents should set limits on this activity. Out of habit, kids will plead that time limits aren't necessary, falsely believing they'll somehow get their to-do lists done later. That's the big lie. After dinner, we know they're running out of energy. They shouldn't put off until then to address their remaining to-do list items.

Engaging needlessly with a time thief because *everybody does it* is a lame excuse. It doesn't fly. I endured many conversations with my kids on this subject. I set rules and limits on their use of electronic devices. I advised them never to cave in to the time demands of friends who wanted to socialize during prime time. Have them kindly explain to their friends that they're busy and will reach out later or in the evening. Practice saying this at home to help them get comfortable saying it to their friends.

I met many successful people while growing up—so long ago that some may think Abe Lincoln was my classmate. Many confessed that when they finally got themselves organized, they suddenly got *smart* too. Struggling kids need to get organized through planning. It's their way out of their mental jails. Planning will make their lives work.

Start with a daily to-do list boiled down from their weekly, monthly, and yearly plans. They should own it. They should doggedly and feverishly work on their to-do lists every day until they get them done. Because once done, they've earned their free time that day. Whew—they can enjoy it without the background noise of unfinished tasks weighing on them: those all-too-familiar feelings of worry, guilt, and frustration. They earned it!

Additionally, kids should start bundling or doing multiple things at once. Show them how to incorporate bundling into their to-do lists to become more efficient. For example, coach them to practice their foreign language vocabulary while folding laundry, cleaning their room, or walking the dog. Challenge them to find even more ways to maximize their time to get things done.

These new skills can turn unproductive time into focused, productive work. It's like putting a car into gear and getting it moving. Fast. Coaching children to use their syllabus and to-do lists will change their worlds. The final win is helping kids learn how to deal with the time thieves. Not only will they find extra time, but they'll also guard it to accomplish more.

Teach your kids that planning what they will do next month is mentally living ahead of themselves. By planning, they begin to visualize themselves doing and experiencing desired outcomes in their future. Carrying out their daily to-do lists allows them to realize those desired outcomes. This makes their lives more predictable, much easier, and more enjoyable.

The Clue Bird changed my life a long time ago when he whispered in my ear, "Don't get frustrated, get organized. Plan your life." That sage-like advice was a blessing, and I hope you'll pass it on to the next generation. By following it, show your kids how to plan and how to gloriously live ahead of themselves.

Don't get frustrated, get organized.
Plan your life.

1- Working hard without focus and lacking a plan is unproductive effort. It's vital to plan, making your hard work productive.

2- Live proactively to remain ahead of yourself. Planning and becoming organized are key to living proactively.

3- A three-year-old's, to-do list, is vastly different from a young adult's; yet the impact on their lives will be quite the same. To-do lists will always be tough and frustrating.

4- Plan your life like you would a vacation, blending careful planning with focused hard work.

5- Bundling or multitasking makes us powerfully productive. Rarely do only one thing at a time.

Lesson 8

Earn It

OUR KIDS CAME Into this world without material possessions. When they were toddlers, our concerns focused on their normal growth and development. For me, it often felt like a full-time job. In subsequent years, they acquired a mix of things, such as a crib, clothes, and a bed. Later, they got jewelry, nicer clothes, countless pairs of sneakers, and sports equipment. They obtained these personal belongings for free because they generated no income.

Starting at birth, kids physically operate and develop on autopilot. As toddlers, their bodies grow and thrive with just air, food, water, and rest. After a few years, they begin actively reacting to whatever is happening in their small world. As parents, we enjoy watching them grow from simply eating and sleeping to exploring their new and wondrous world.

Over time, their lives become busier and more difficult to manage. They begin to change into young adults. As a dad, my personal dilemma hinged on figuring out how to get my kids to give up their childlike ways. I expected them to do so automatically—but they didn't. To my disbelief, they wanted to stay emotionally and mentally where they were, even as they physically grew into young adults.

As children move on to middle school, they face new and troubling issues with ever-increasing frequency. They suddenly have to manage their days instead of just doing what they want. Additionally, schoolwork gets harder and harder. Like many parents, I grew frustrated trying to get my kids to act like the adults they were becoming. My efforts focused on teaching them to adopt a new mindset: work hard, always do what they must do first, and begin earning what they wanted and desired. Not all kids will do it.

One group of kids will openly and willingly adapt to this new mind-set. They stop wasting time and willingly give up their haphazard, "only do what I want to do" mentality—though they wouldn't have known any other way. With effort, they become organized students, steadily working through their to-do lists each day. Then, with minor adjustments to those lists, their new approach puts them on track to reaching their goals. They become excellent students.

Another group of kids will choose to do what they must do first, but only on a so-so basis. Despite all efforts, they lag in becoming true believers. They remain lukewarm on the idea of always doing what they must do first. It takes more time for this group to fully grasp what's required to adopt this new mindset. Their progress in school is half-baked or haphazard. Sometimes they get organized and follow their plans—other times, they don't. Often, their to-do lists are incomplete or ignored altogether. It shows in their grades.

These kids will likely complete projects late, as their progress is often unpredictable. Mostly, they remain average students. Just like with their schoolwork, their performance in other activities is hit or miss. In sports, for example, they can be hot, cold, or spotty. Most become practice players because their poor work ethic holds them back. This group struggles to put in the work and earn it. Generally, they remain average at best. No one wants their kid stuck in a group needlessly prolonged into a life of being average.

Lastly, the remaining group includes those kids who refuse to adapt to the new mindset. Fortunately, this is a relatively small group. By choice, these kids continue to whimsically do whatever they want to do most of the time, and this often ends badly. The major difference between these three emerging groups lies in their ownership of a new mindset.

They either fully decide to always do first what they must, followed by what they want to do in their leisure time, or they don't. It all boils down to a simple choice: to do the work or not. Working hard at something is earning it. Every parent should work hard to ensure their kids are in the first group.

I must confess, for a while, I was in the last group. Growing up, I was the baby in the family and liked my grandmother's older siblings doing everything for me. I got spoiled, becoming somewhat lazy. Very lazy. Throughout middle school, my friends and I did only what we wanted to do. We scraped by with minimal effort in practically every aspect of our lives, thinking we were smart. We weren't. I knew soon after entering high school—back when they had just invented the steam locomotive. At least, it seems that long ago. It wasn't.

The problem was that high school was way beyond my maturity level. I fell far behind and felt lost. My memory of my predicament is that I was, at best, very average in practically everything. I had nothing in my heart I wanted to do, except play sports. I was lethargic, miserable, and longing for the good old days back in elementary school when life was easy. The academic eligibility needed to play sports was pressing me to do something significantly different in the classroom.

Worried sick about my academic wipeout, I fell asleep on the couch. In a dream, a little bird stood on my shoulder, whispering, "Grow up, embrace adulthood. Work hard, earn it all." Startled awake, I sprang up. I sat there for a long time thinking about the message.

Right away, I knew it was eerily truthful and full of wisdom. Instead of ignoring it until morning, out of desperation I embraced it right then, thinking it might help me. After thinking about the first part, "grow up," I thought it was obvious. I hadn't done it, yet.

Deciphering the message

Pondering the "grow up" part, I consulted with myself, washed in absolute truthfulness, and fully committed to owning my problem. The overwhelming evidence piled up fast. My life was going nowhere. The problem was, even though I had grown into the size of a large man, I was still acting mentally and emotionally like I was in the sixth grade.

Feeling deeply ashamed of my behavior, I finally owned it. I vowed on the spot to change and change quickly. I realized I had lost a lot of ground by prolonging my childish behavior. I needed to make it up and prove to myself I was a gifted person with a good future.

The next part of the little bird's advice was to embrace adulthood. After thinking about it, I reflected on past conversations with my uncle Jerry. He had joined the military a few years earlier, and I had immense fondness and respect for him. I had watched him shift from being like

I was at that time into a professional soldier. While home on leave, he would visit with me for hours, sharing the new insights he'd learned from his military training. He had given me great advice—advice I hadn't embraced.

For example, Uncle Jerry once asked if I knew what it took for him to become a professional soldier. I didn't. After an awkward moment of silence, he said, "It was my decision." He repeated this to me several times, adding that he learned the hard way: everything in life starts with a decision. "Decisions change your life," he said.

Ironically, he had also discovered that just deciding was the hardest part of changing his life. He explained that after making his decision, it became a labor of love to work hard to become excellent at what he had chosen to be.

While in the service, my uncle stayed in shape and "squared away," which took hours of personal work and development. During that time, he worked harder than ever to be his best, not only for himself but for others ranking above and below him.

My uncle added they depended on him being a victor, not a victim. He said the instructors taught him to take excellent care of himself so he could take care of others if needed. He also told me to start thinking about others, especially my grandmother.

My uncle learned from his trainers and superiors to be early, fully prepared, and always do the right thing. The right thing meant always doing what was needed or had to be done first—completely done, no matter how hard it was! In time, he willingly and enthusiastically did the hard work he had to do.

This made him dependable for the first time in his life. Being dependable made him feel like a leader. He explained that he had learned to lead himself first, knowing that only then did he earn the right to lead others. Over and over, he stressed, "You have to earn it. You have to earn everything in life."

During one of our conversations, Uncle Jerry said, "I only wish someone had told me this earlier, when I was growing up." He believed it would've changed his life sooner. The service taught him to embrace being a responsible adult—not just for himself, but for others too. Right then I decided to emulate Uncle Jerry.

Lastly, the little bird advised me, "Work hard, earn it all." That sank into me at a gut level. Many times, my uncle stressed working hard was *the key*. "Only little kids get things given to them. To earn it, you must work hard for it," he told me.

In one conversation, he even admitted he had just faked his way through high school. "Sound familiar?" he asked back then. Embarrassed and feeling like a little kid, I had to admit he had just described me. He'd been self-absorbed, selfishly doing the minimum to get by. I was doing the same. Still, I hadn't done anything about it.

Applying the message

Thinking about my conversations with Uncle Jerry made me wonder why I hadn't fully understood his advice years before my Clue Bird dream. The strange little bird whispered in my ear practically the same amazing advice. Connecting the two helped me understand the advice. I was finally ready to use it.

I began working hard at being the best football player and teammate I could be. That included extra physical training, and even doing cone and ladder drills in my backyard, tearing up the sod. Whatever it took, I worked hard with focus for the first time. With my new attitude, I had finally *earned* my spot on our team. I felt like I belonged because I had earned it.

In the classroom, I did the same. I became a "front row" student, joined study groups, and laid out my schedules to start living ahead of myself. For the first time, I worked hard and smart—with focus and a plan. I was surprised how easy the classes became for me. While learning to apply what the Clue Bird advised, I remembered asking my grandmother why other people had nice things and we didn't. She told me, "Stay in your own backyard."

Later she sat me down to explain what she meant. She insisted everyone should view their life as a little house with a small fenced-in backyard. With that understanding, the house, yard, and all its possessions represent your life up to that moment. She told me to focus on taking care of my own backyard. She assured me doing so would help me live a bountiful life.

All I had to do was care for my imaginary house—mow and trim the grass, water the plants and flowers, prune the trees, wash off the patio, paint the fence, make repairs, straighten the chairs, and on and on. No easy task, but it's the effort needed to care for our backyards.

My grandmother said, "Consider how the work you do in your own backyard involves always doing the things you must do first. When you do that, your backyard will be an excellent yard—or life." A life well lived. She suggested looking at some of my friends, pointing out how a few were still running on their old playbook of only doing what they felt like and putting off what they must do.

They were proof that being lazy, self-centered, and irresponsible is not a winning formula. My grandmother said she could easily see the terrible condition of their lives because of their poor choices.

Additionally, my grandmother told me to never investigate a neighbor's backyard! "Don't ever throw your leg over their fence, and never jump into your neighbor's backyard or life," she said. According to my grandmother, what other people's yards looked like was none of my business.

She warned me not to ever look into or step next door to try helping others with their yards. She told me they most assuredly didn't ask for my help, nor did they seek out my expertise. "They, like you, probably feel their yard or life is just fine. So, don't waste time in a neighbor's backyard. It robs you of the time you could use tending to your own yard." She taught me to just take care of myself because it's a full-time job.

Following her direction, I was to let others do the same with their yards. My grandmother believed another reason not to investigate someone's yard was that you might discover it's a lot nicer than yours, and it could cause you grief, pain, or envy. It's so easy to look at someone else's yard or life and feel envy or jealousy when you see others have developed their backyards or lives far better. While it might be natural to feel that way, the best response is to always feel gratitude and happiness for your friend's gifts and successes.

It's about developing the mindset that you, too, can and may someday possess those things. With your own hard work, you'll earn it. Instead of feeling bad with envy and jealousy, feel grateful. Know that by working harder in your own backyard, those things may be in your life as well, with focused effort. Just earn it.

Remembering her advice was eerily like the advice of the Clue Bird and my uncle Jerry. It was sage-like advice from two different people at different times in my life. When the Clue Bird jolted me into an awakening with his message, I was finally ready to understand and use it.

Be ready to earn it

What my grandmother said to me made sense. Teaching kids to stay in their own backyard and always do what they must do first is paramount. Every kid has to learn to focus on themselves. My kids often told me everybody does this or that, or that they wanted to do what someone else was doing. I responded by telling them to mind their own business—to stay in their own backyards.

I taught my children to be like my uncle Jerry. Dependable. Others will not only trust your kids, but they will also want to emulate them. Kids should know that everything in life is defined by the amount of work they put into it. They must follow their plan in their little fenced-in backyard. They must tend to it, always doing what they must, putting in the work and effort to make and keep it excellent.

The nonstop increase in complexity as kids age drives them to a moment where they have to make a choice: the choice to get organized by adopting a new mindset of strictly doing first what they have to do, then doing things they want to do. That subtle shift will allow them to either become adept and skillful at getting lots of work done in relatively short periods of time, or to face lives that become chaotic and difficult to manage.

With coaching, your child must choose. The choice they make will ultimately place them into one of the three groups we discussed earlier. I knew what group my kids were in, and I'll bet you dads want to determine where your kids will end up as well. Here's one way you could try. Every day, have them make two separate lists.

The first list should include everything they have to do that day. The second list should have all the things they want to do. Encourage them to stick with the first list until they've completed every item. Only then will they have earned the right to move on to the second list.

Adapting to this took longer than I imagined, but the system finally worked for my kids. It will likely work for yours too. Once they develop mentally and emotionally, they will act like young adults. It's a challenge to be won while raising them, not after they become adults. Show your child how to embrace adulthood, work hard, and be smart. Just earn it.

Grow up. Embrace adulthood. Work hard to earn it all.

1- Nothing in life is free. Earn it with planning and focused hard work.

2- Aimlessly working hard may prove frustratingly unproductive. Doing the things you must do first is productive hard work with focus and a plan.

3- Continue to develop mentally and emotionally into adulthood. This is a challenge to be won while young, not after becoming an adult.

4- Telling someone something once or twice may not be enough. It may take untold conversations over a long period of time to fully understand and use something.

5- Earn attention with hard work. Eliminate attention seeking behavior, and always get attention for the right reasons.

LESSON 9

GOAL SETTING

WE'VE ALL HAD MOMENTS with our kids when we noticed they were confused, frustrated, and overwhelmed about life. It feels like they get almost nothing done. Worse, they're always late, falling behind in both school and sports while staying remarkably busy. It's like the world is operating at a faster speed, and they don't know how to catch up.

If a kid can't keep up, we must worry about how they'll ever be able to catch up moving forward. Having well-meaning caretakers and various family members assist them by doing too many things for them provides temporary help. But we know propping them up temporarily is not the desired long-term answer. To make progress, kids have to become more skillful at goal setting.

Observe the children around you. Note those kids who turn in their assignments not just on time but even early. What about your kids' teammates? Which ones show up to practice early? Do they also have their needed equipment and display boundless energy at practice? Perhaps some of your kids' friends personally help their classmates, or even your kid, with their schoolwork. Many of these kids may also join numerous clubs and earn straight A's. What makes this possible?

I often observed my kids' friends in this way, and the differences disturbed me. I wondered, if their friends could do this, why couldn't they? What are my kids lacking, I often worried. I decided to observe them for an entire week. Afterwards, I sadly realized they had no plan, and they worked hard but haphazardly. They didn't get much done with their spurious efforts. They were falling behind. I asked them about their hopes and dreams. They had big dreams, and I wanted them to accomplish them.

They were both in middle school, and it was time for them to learn goal setting with a commitment to focus on hard work. Middle school is a unique time for kids as they transition from elementary school into a more complex world. The pace is faster, more demanding, and the assigned schoolwork grows. Suddenly, kids are dealing with harder academics, plus extracurricular activities and more chores at home. Worse, middle school mixes hormones with algebra.

They can no longer keep up by just reacting. They need a new way to get ahead of their responsibilities. Reacting means always being behind, which causes kids to complain. They work hard but with no focus or plan. They resemble a juggler who is surprisingly good at juggling three balls, but as more and more balls are added, his performance ultimately results in failure. Some kids are in the same predicament. They need to develop new skills to adapt.

If your kids are behind in school or frustrated because they don't know what to do differently to change their situation, perhaps they need to learn goal setting. Setting goals can help them focus. With focus, they'll work more productively to get things done. Many children struggle to keep up in school.

They're all in the same boat—struggling, frustrated, and miserable because their lives are not nearly as successful as they should or could be. Instead of focusing on fixing their problem, they predictably only alibi it. Sometimes, they assume successful students are probably just smarter, more gifted, or whatever label they choose to tag them with.

We know that's not the real difference. The difference is some kids haven't learned how to manage their schoolwork. When I was back in school, before electricity was invented, I had a heck of a time with my schoolwork.

During my school days, I was needlessly average. Even though I was just as smart as my classmates, I was always behind in school. For some reason, I struggled with my studies and sports. Out of necessity, I wasn't even a good classmate. I got so far behind I had no time to be anyone's real friend. My predicament really depressed me.

One afternoon during a short nap, a magical little bird whispered ever so clearly, "Choose what you want, set goals, achieve with consistent effort, doing what's needed." The dream woke me up. I sat at my desk to write down what I heard in my strange dream. Somehow, I just knew this was great advice.

Deciphering the message

To make sure I got things going on the right track, I considered doing this work with my parents or even with some friends, but I decided it was best to do it alone. Doing it alone, I sought clarity and honesty with myself. It didn't take very long, because, in my heart, my current frustration was telegraphing that something needed to change.

First, I wondered, what exactly does "Choose what you want" mean? I decided it meant I had to get clear and decide what I wanted to accomplish. To get started, I wrote down the things I wanted to work on. I addressed grades, sports activities, physical development, extracurricular interests, clubs, and new interests. These are just some of the ideas I put down.

I also wrote them down in pencil, keeping my large eraser handy. Sitting there, I tried to figure out what I wanted in life. I was just a kid. For example, at one point, I wanted to be a rodeo star just because I had a big hat. But right then, I focused only on what I wanted out of school. This included certain classes, sports, music, drama, clubs, and getting the best grades possible. All of this gave me a complete list of what I wanted to achieve.

"Set goals" was the next thing the Clue Bird said to me back then. Of course, graduating from high school was one of the things I wanted. I wrote: "graduate from high school" on my paper, visualizing the actual accomplishment of that goal in my mind. Next, I worked backward from my expected graduation date to that day, filling in the details that came to mind.

From there, I focused on the last piece of advice from the Clue Bird: "Doing what's needed." I didn't really know what was needed right then, so I broke everything down to get a step-by-step view of what it would take to meet my goal to graduate from high school. I thought about the grades I wanted to have, as I was on sports teams year-round and wanted to go to college.

With a good list of what I wanted to do and my main goal to graduate from high school, I figured all I needed to do was work hard with a determined mindset to do what the Clue Bird told me.

Applying the message

I decided I had nothing to lose by putting in consistent effort. I didn't just try it; I had been so miserable, I decided to absolutely follow this advice like an obsession every day, for lack of a better idea, to see what would happen. Basically, with the help of my teachers, I learned that goal attainment means figuring out the intermediate details needed to get to the finish line.

What I learned helped me set goals with trackable milestones. For example, let's say your kid sets a goal of bench pressing two hundred pounds. Sounds like a big goal. He sets out to the gym full of enthusiasm to lift weights in pursuit of that goal. Several weeks go by. To his dismay, he discovers he has lost ground, and his goal is now even farther away. Like most people, he decides to give up or quit. He will run on his *story*: goal setting doesn't work. It's a waste of time. However, setting up this goal incorrectly is what caused the failure.

It's simple. Setting up a goal is claiming your future. You can say, "I bench press 200 pounds." After that, you work backward, providing the details and timeframes. Getting a list of milestones for weight-lifting might start with learning the basics, then building strength by increasing weights slowly and doing bench presses at least twice a week. Without exception, every goal needs a timeframe to go with each milestone. Together, they provide a roadmap for how to accomplish that goal. Doing all of these things will help kids reach their goals.

Any kid could improve their life with goals. Some time ago, a successful friend shared his secret to excelling in school. First, he said he figured out what caused years of difficulty by accident. Out of frustration, he became extremely organized.

The more organized he got, the smarter he got too—it was just that simple. Although he told me he was probably of average intelligence, he held two PhDs. To his surprise, being organized made him very efficient, which led him to start feeling smart for the first time in his life. His new excellent grades reinforced his beliefs.

Another friend shared a story about a talk he had with his older brother. He said that one night his brother walked into his room and started messing with his pet gerbil, Sammy. The gerbil stayed on his desk in a little cage that had a flywheel for it to exercise on. His brother said, "Sitting here watching Sammy, I'm noticing he runs around aimlessly, going from one thing to the next with no plan. No offense, but your actions resemble your gerbil's.

He gets on his flywheel, expends lots of energy, and runs and runs, going nowhere." My friend said his brother looked him in the eye, saying, "You practically do the same." Then his brother told him, "That's why you get little accomplished while being busy, needlessly burning lots of energy." Hearing this inspired my friend to get organized.

I agree with my friend. Getting organized makes you smarter. It means getting more done and avoiding needless mistakes, setbacks, and errors. It also makes kids feel smarter, as their lives become more manageable. Basically, living without goals or plans is like being in a boat without a rudder, furiously paddling nonstop, going nowhere.

Getting organized and setting goals adds a rudder to your life. That's why showing your kids how to set goals and do what it takes to attain them is so important. It might be painful for some kids to switch to living with a plan, but it's better than acting like Sammy the gerbil.

Plans have power

Have you ever noticed how certain kids go humming along, being successful in practically every aspect of their lives while showing no apparent stress? They also seem happy, content, relaxed, and a pleasure to be around. They never seem rushed, worried, or in a personal jam. These kids are composed, successful, kind, and liked by others. If your kids struggle with getting things done, perhaps they can ask those kids how they do it.

Years ago, when I compared my kids to successful students, it seemed as if they were missing something or not getting something. I realized they needed to learn goal setting and focused hard work. They had to learn how to become proactive and no longer just reactive. When planning, have your child visualize their goal along with the date of its accomplishment.

From there, have them work their way back to the present, filling in as much detail and as many intermediate goals as possible. This builds a detailed roadmap, getting them successfully from here to there while keeping them on track and within their desired time frame.

The next thing the Clue Bird told me, way back when they were just inventing the automobile, was to work "with consistent effort." What does that mean? Well, it goes back to hard work and effort. To do it, you need some basic time management skills. It's very simple. It means always working to achieve your chosen goals and sticking with them.

Having the right effort is a good first step to doing what's needed. As we grow, many goals change, and they may need adjustments. That's why kids should write down their goals in a way that allows for easy changes, such as using a notebook or worksheet they can revise as they grow.

With my kids, we worked at the dining room table. Using pencils and lots of paper, they wrote down everything they thought they wanted to accomplish. Then we shortened their lists. We made it a lighthearted exercise filled with laughter. It was an incredibly good start.

Let's continue with our example goal, "graduating from high school." Their fill-in items should be both detailed and organized by year. For each year until graduation, they should list their classes, desired grades, extracurricular activities, jobs, and so forth, providing needed detail to the intermediate steps to keep them on track.

Getting it done means kids have to work every day like a person possessed to achieve their dreams. Fortunately, goal setting is easy. The hard part is the driven effort. It's practically impossible to achieve your goals without consistent effort. Children can't just do the drill of writing down a goal with a bunch of intermediate steps and then set it aside. They must remember that early in their lives they were given gifts with no effort required on their part. Now, they must earn a lot of it on their own. This is a key step.

Align their goals within the time frame they picked for themselves. Help them get started, and they will be well on their way to a successful life. Teach them to always do what they must do first, not what they want to do. Try this exercise with your child. Have them carefully observe the successful people they encounter, asking, "Is the mindset of doing what's needed present in their lives?" Have them look at their successful friends. Do they have specific goals packed with considerable detail, keeping them on track? Do they operate with a consistent, driven effort? I bet they do.

There are many kids who have already figured things out. They consistently work daily, doing what they must do first. This allows them time to do what they want and to enjoy their hard-earned leisure time. It means they successfully did the things they were responsible for that day. We must stress to kids the importance of fully honoring the habit of doing what's needed.

If they don't, goal setting will prove to be a waste of their time. Their lives will not change. Every child has to start doing what they must get done first. Only then do they earn the right to do whatever they wish in their leisure time. Therefore, guide them to decide what they want. Help them map out their goals and fill in as much detail as possible.

We need to be aware of another problem related to goal setting. It's goal overloading—having too many goals. It doesn't work because it dilutes effort. If kids have too many goals, it prevents them from focusing on any of them. They get nothing done.

In these cases, the frustration can be as bad as before, or maybe even worse. When this happens, even setting goals might create increased effort with little to show because there's only so much time in a day. Something must give. Remember, success means avoiding further frustration. That's why we need to help kids pick a reasonable number of goals. Kids must be driven by their dreams.

Help your child set goals and ensure those goals support their dreams. Teach them to strive, never giving up until they get what they want most. Doing this will keep them from mimicking Sammy the gerbil, running nowhere on their flywheels. Instead, you'll watch your child mold themselves into the proud and successful person they were born to become.

Getting organized and setting goals simply changed the trajectory of my life from being average to extraordinary. I didn't need a brain transplant after all, as the real transplant I needed back then was simply to use my newfound focused efforts. Heed the Clue Bird's sage-like advice. It's timeless. It worked for me, and it will work for your kids.

Choose what you want, set goals, & achieve with consistent effort, doing what's needed.

1- Always do what you must do first.

2- Goal setting can guide you to working toward something.

3- Live proactively working toward something, using goal setting with focused hard work.

4- The hardest part of goal setting is maintaiing the prolonged consistent effort needed to achieve your goals. Consistent effort, means working every day like a person possessed, achieving dreams or goals.

5- Your goals are your dreams. Fall in love with them and then strive for your dreams with consistent effort, never giving up on you.

LESSON 10

COLLEGE OR TRADE SCHOOL

AFTER MY KIDS FINISHED high school, I talked with them about their upcoming plans to transition into college. I felt happy about their graduation but with trepidation because they thought high school was a piece of cake. They wanted to move on to even greater challenges without making any changes because they did great in high school.

The angst I felt was because my kids claimed they were successful. Although they graduated with honors, they should have realized they had merely accomplished this by coasting through, playing their kid-like minimal effort game. I felt like screaming. I worried because I believed they had been lulled to sleep.

Being easy, high school did them no favors. Maybe they didn't realize it because running their kid-like minimal effort game was the only game they knew. I felt the need to teach them a better game. I knew from experience, moving on to college or trade school with the wrong attitude or work ethic might not pan out for them. I asked them if they thought their overconfidence going into college was in their best interests, or were they just nervously whistling by the graveyard?

When I discussed moving on from high school to college, trade school, or the military with my kids, I reminded them I went to college way back when. Even though we studied under candlelight, I found advanced education significantly more difficult than high school. I explained that advanced learning might be a quantum leap forward in both academic and personal growth, one that would require them to master focused hard work.

I knew my kids' plan to quickly move on to the next chapter without reflection wasn't going to work for them. "Take it from me," I said, admitting I had acted very much like both of them in high school.

Sadly, I wish I had accomplished more when I was there. Looking back, I regret my attitude because I was just cheating myself.

I played the game of doing the absolute least at the last minute. My stingy attitude made me a master at the game. I barely did what I had to do to get by. I was needlessly average and a borderline success for most of my time in high school. It hit me hard one night when the magical little clue bird landed on my shoulder in a dream. I heard him say very clearly, "Victims do the least, while victors do the maximum, so which one are you?"

The dream was so realistic, it woke me up. I grabbed a piece of paper and wrote down what the little bird said to me. It took practically no time for me to understand it. With my new perspective, I instantly realized how foolish it was to live a minimal-effort life. I felt embarrassed and disappointed in myself, as I knew I was better than average.

Deciphering the message

I thought about each part of what the little bird said. "Victims do the least," described me in four words. I reflected on many areas of my life, realizing that for no apparent reason, I always did the least in practically every aspect of my very average life—as a son, sibling, friend, teammate, or classmate.

I surmised I took pride in getting away with doing the least at everything. I thought it proved I was smart. I wasn't smart. Doing the least probably created my many needless problems, and those problems made my life miserable, frustrating, and very average. I was gradually becoming a victim because of my choices.

For years, I acted like I was on the bottom side of a teeter-totter playing on a playground. While sitting on the low side of the teeter-totter, I acted like a kid. I did very little for myself, always doing the minimum and at the last minute—selfish and effortless, refusing to help myself. That day, I made the decision to push up to the high side of the teeter-totter. Suddenly, I wanted to act more grown up.

In a moment of clarity, I decided to change my mindset to always doing the maximum at whatever I was doing. I had a new, focused hard work attitude. From this new height, I saw the world better and formulated my dreams. I promised myself to apply one hundred percent to every task, whether big or small. That was what the Clue Bird meant by saying, "While victors do the maximum." I decided to become a victor no matter what it took. I was tired of the rat race, disappointment, and angst of doing the minimum and needlessly being in the bottom half of everything. I was speeding down the road to victimhood. That singular decision was mine alone.

I answered the Clue Bird's question, "So which one are you?" My answer—victor. Then I changed from being a victim with one simple decision to work hard toward my dreams. With that singular decision, pursuing my dreams with a hard-work attitude became a labor of love, as I worked toward something instead of just at something. The change was refreshing. I quickly became successful in high school and beyond.

Applying the message

In high school, kids can slack off and still earn good grades while doing the minimum because teachers often bend the rules to help them out. But coddling doesn't prepare them for what's coming. Soon after my kids graduated, we reviewed their high school experience during a family-style discussion.

Sitting around the dining room table for hours, we looked back at their experience. We discussed that they needed to give up their familiar, kid-like, minimal-effort approach to life prior to moving on to college, trade school, or the military, to avoid a potential disaster.

Taking the time to review what your children might do in high school is a good way to coach them to avoid having a minimal-effort approach of doing the least amount of work possible. If you do, your kids will spend their time really learning something.

There are many things we can teach our kids to do to get the best out of high school. One way is joining a study group. Collectively, students might vow to squeeze as much out of each class as possible. Individually, they could meet with their teachers during office hours to discuss their planned progress in each class. They could also ask for additional readings that might add perspective to the class as well.

What about trying out for a school play? I pushed my kids to try out. They didn't. That would have been a growth decision for them. I know because I once jokingly tried out for a play with a friend back in high school. Shockingly, I earned a part! I discovered rehearsals were both time-consuming but enjoyable. While in the play, I met a completely new group of students I would never have met otherwise.

Trying out for a play can give kids a chance to become proficient at something completely new to them. For one thing, they must face the absolute inner terror of performing in front of peers, family, and friends. Encourage your child to try out for many things so that they might have as many experiences as possible and meet many new people along the way.

During our meeting, we discussed minimal effort. We also reviewed my kids' recent high school sports careers. Lucky for them, what was difficult for others was easy for them. That gift of natural talent, sadly, played perfectly into their minimal-effort way of thinking. With little effort, they made the team and could slide by.

It was no sweat for my kids to make the baseball team or to become starters with minimal effort. They showed up, practiced, and played in their varsity games. However, I asked them to consider what their minimal-effort attitude cost them.

It reminded me of my old friend, Todd, who earned a college football scholarship. While reminiscing about his high school days, he recalled being the biggest and naturally strongest player on the team. During required weightlifting, he would just skate because, without trying, he was recognized as the strongest player in the gym.

He remembered being a star athlete and excelling in high school with minimal effort. After playing in college, he was so ashamed of his lack of effort in high school. Regrettably, he took advantage of how easy it was for him.

Todd believed high school being easy was not a gift. It was a curse. Todd went off to college on a scholarship. Unlike high school, he found every aspect of college difficult. It was so difficult that he almost didn't make it. Classes when combined with working out and playing football required focused hard work. If Todd had increased his motivation and effort back in high school, he could have gone from naturally good to extraordinary. With a changed attitude he could have been even more prepared for college.

During my high school review with my kids, I asked them, "How do you think it would sound if we were to candidly talk to your old classmates about how you were back then? Were you in student government, an officer in any club, captain of any team?"

Out of the hundreds of students, how many would they consider as friends? If the answer is maybe ten out of hundreds, consider what a pathetically small percentage of the student population they interacted with. Some kids don't get out of their inner circles to grow socially.

Hopefully, kids learn the effort they put out always comes back to them in spades. Sure, sports come to mind, but taking classes outside of their interests, sitting with a different group of students during lunch, taking a foreign language, being in a play, and always being friendly are examples of extra effort. Doing these things will significantly add to a kid's experience. Not doing such things robs them of diverse experiences during that time of their lives.

In contrast, we discussed how living maxed out is a much easier life, allowing them to eliminate a lot of hand-wringing, pain, arguments, and just being ordinary. I asked them, "Who wants to be just ordinary? Do you? Do you want to live an ordinary life? Do you want to live day in and day out doing the least you can each day? Is it cool and clever?" No, it's not, and they knew it.

Doing the minimum would have caused them to spend far more effort just ending up being ordinary at best. It's like a guy sitting in front of a fireplace saying, "Give me heat and I'll put in some wood." No, you physically put in the wood and then stoke the fire to stay warm all night. The only change here is the wood, which represents effort. It's harder to stay cold than it is to put in a little effort on the front end to become and remain comfortable.

Mindset makes the difference

Shooting ducks in a barrel doesn't make you Annie Oakley. It simply makes you look good while hiding your weaknesses. Being excellent at anything easy, such as high school, doesn't necessarily prove your excellence. Before kids go off to college, I suggest parents work with them to set goals based on their dreams. Have them promise to always do what they must or need to do first and only then do what they want to do in their well-earned leisure time.

Watching kids move onto college, trade school, or the military doesn't end our job as parents. We must nudge them to keep growing, mentally and emotionally. If a kid has lived their life doing the minimum, only reacting to life, and living without a plan or focus, things will be harder for them after high school. Whatever they do in the future, we must teach them to strive and squeeze the maximum out of everything.

What will be your kid's story? Will it be a continuation of doing the minimum? Will they just slide through college like they did in high school, with a few friends, easy classes, doing the absolute minimum to just pass, so they can get their degree? Or will they choose to expand their interests, reach out, grow, force themselves to make new friends, and get the most out of it?

Have your kids decide they're going to honor themselves by making the firm decision to give up their kid-stuff mentality and move into a new adult mentality of living their lives with the focused maximum effort required to attain their dreams.

I warned my kids that this new chapter of their lives could brutally highlight weaknesses they were not aware of. I also reminded them that high school was free. It cost them nothing but their time. Since people often value things based on their personal costs, my kids acted accordingly, exerting minimal effort. I told them college or trade schools are expensive. I encouraged them to apply themselves in earnest.

From personal experience, I was fully aware of this major change my kids were unknowingly facing. They weren't. They were confident and even smug about their upcoming college experience. They thought college would be just more of the same.

Relaxing in the den one night, I told them the story of Jim, my best friend in high school. He was a year ahead of me and I looked up to him because he had earned several varsity letters, had great grades, and was well-liked. Plus, it was a lot of fun being around him. Prior to leaving for college, his proud parents gave him a going away party. They called it his "Off to College" party. Most of his friends and fellow students attended. I went.

During his party, the chatter was all about, "Can't wait... it will be a piece of cake. Parties and social life with no parents around and no curfews. Heaven." There was talk about finally being grown up and able to do as one pleased, and on and on. Jim went off to college. When he returned for the holidays, I eagerly went to his house to catch up with my *college friend*. Something seemed drastically wrong. In his bedroom, he confessed he had flunked out of school.

When Jim arrived on campus, he partied. He often missed his early morning classes and had even gotten way behind in his homework. He couldn't get organized. Jim had done the same in high school, but the teachers would bend the rules helping him out of a jam.

In college, he found out the hard way—they don't care. He explained how in college, it didn't matter if you missed class, missed homework, failed a test, or got sick—they don't care. It's on you. He admitted even though he did well in high school, he wasn't prepared for college because he had been coddled too much by his family and teachers.

Jim learned the hard way why just doing the minimum doesn't work, and that you can't ever get behind. He got behind and couldn't catch up. What he shared was tearful, gut-level honesty. Parents know children are different when they finally shed this attitude, which takes little or no effort. Jim didn't do it. When a child makes the decision to give up thinking like a kid, they quickly morph into a new mature attitude of "I can."

The pursuit of their hopes and dreams will create the inner motivation for them to push forward no matter what. In the flying game, we call it "setting your hair on fire." It means wanting to do something so badly you're willing to die for it. To be on fire like that, kids need to identify the hopes and dreams in their hearts.

Coach your children to enrich themselves by becoming doers. Show them how to become a "first in line" type of person who constantly resets their goals higher and higher as they attain them. Teach them to apply themselves in earnest by working hard, learning as much as possible to help others around them, and to stretch themselves out of their comfort zones.

I recommend parents review their children's lives in a family discussion. After reviewing my kids' high school days, there was a good feeling around the kitchen table. We honestly discussed the last four years of their lives, and it was an excellent experience of respectful give and take. Telling them the story of my friend Jim, who flunked out of college after being successful in high school, made them sit up and think.

My old friend Todd's story also had a significant impact on them. To wrap up our discussion, I summarized how having an easy time in high school had allowed them to be successful with minimal effort. By the end of our discussion, I could tell my kids were starting to change their minds. With hugs and handshakes, they agreed to make an adult, hard-work ethic their new mantra. They both went on to college and were very successful. Additionally, their entire lives are extraordinary, and they are teaching this hard work mantra to their children.

Industrious kids shouldn't look at college as a four-year program. College will be approximately 1,460 days of their lives sewn together. Just like someone's grandmother who sews quilts, they're going to stitch together 1,460 days into a beautiful quilt.

Help your kids put thought and effort into it. Let them get their money's worth and more. One day, when they've finished college and reflect on their experience, let's hope it won't be a repeat of their high school days. Don't let that happen to your kids.

Victims do the least, while victors do the maximum. So which are you?

1- Choose to be a victor. Willingly and aggressively morph into a new adult-like focused-hard work approach to life to continue achieving.

2- Convert your dreams into the physical world. Apply maximum effort doing whatever it takes to finally experience them.

3- Do you want to be ordinary or live an ordinary life? Do you want to always do the least? Is that smart or clever? No, it's not and we all know it. Choose to grow up to become the victor you were born to be.

4- Employ a maximum effort approach to life. Decide to work hard making the most out of everything you do.

5- At college you will sew approximately 1460 days into a quilt of your life. Make it a beautiful quilt with your focused hard work efforts.

Lesson 11

Personal Finances

I HAD MANY DISCUSSIONS about money with my kids. Helping them understand personal finances started early with piggy banks. Once they were old enough, I offered an allowance that they could earn by doing assigned chores. When they received their allowance, they enthusiastically deposited the coins into their little banks. After some time, we broke open the piggy banks. Their surprise and glee spread across the room as they eagerly counted what they had saved.

As they grew older, they did more chores at home to earn larger sums of money. This process morphed into doing work for others: mowing lawns, paper routes, washing cars, and minor repair jobs. However, during this transition period, it became more difficult to get them to save their money. It seemed the more they made, the less they wanted to save. They would whine, "I worked hard for that money, and I want to spend it."

Like so many parents, I spent a considerable amount of time explaining the importance of saving a portion of their money. I suggested they save a small amount and spend the rest as they pleased. They had earned it, and I wanted them to enjoy it too. The problem was their *spend it all* mentality. They wanted nothing to do with keeping their money for later. I understood that mindset.

During my high school days, back when they had just invented railroads, I took a job to make a little extra money. I selfishly told myself that since I earned it, why not spend it? All of it. I figured that since I had worked hard for the money, it should be mine and mine alone. Then I had an encounter with my so-called friend Ted, who lived next door to us. I had helped him get hired at the restaurant where I was working.

His life wasn't predictable, successful, or trouble-free. He was always trying to borrow money from me, and he never paid back what I loaned him. He was at best, an average to below average classmate of mine. One day, my coworkers were talking about how he tried to get additional hours at work. I went over to Ted and asked, "Why do you want to work so much?" He said he needed the money.

Later, I found out about him buying another classmate's old car, which was a real clunker. He bought it on credit, promising to pay back so much a week until he paid off the loan. Another thing, Ted was also quite the dresser. Unlike me, he wore the latest cool stuff but his entire world blew up when his car broke down.

He couldn't get to work, got fired, and was already failing two classes because of the workload he carried at his job. Ted hadn't saved any money because he thought he was just too smart to ever have to get through a fix like this. He didn't see it coming. He just crashed and burned, as they say.

My uncle Jerry, who was home on military leave at the time, had just told me that if you observe anything bad, always learn from other people's mistakes. He said it was the way to learn a valuable life lesson on the cheap. Some days after, I spent hours thinking about some of the issues Ted brought on himself. I wondered what safeguards I could set up to avoid getting into a predicament like Ted's. I concluded it was his spending habits that did him in.

Then one night, I was awakened from a dream by the presence of a beautiful bird standing on my shoulder. As clear as anything, he said, "Work hard, always pay yourself first, and prosper."

Deciphering the message

Over the next few days, I couldn't get the image of the Clue Bird out of my brain. He was a beautiful male cardinal. I could see him in amazing detail. What he said so calmly kept me thinking about it for hours. Analyzing, "work hard," was no problem for me to understand. Thinking about it further, however, I also considered that "work hard" also meant to always be honorable to an employer. This meant I had to always do my job in a way I could be proud of, work to get along with coworkers, and be a dependable worker.

I also figured out what the Clue Bird meant by "always pay yourself first." I had never thought of it that way. As a spender, I paid everyone else first—for things I had already bought. Then I could keep what was left—if anything. That seemed unfair because it was my money in the first place. Thinking about "paying yourself first," I realized I needed to limit my spending in order to pay myself first and add to my savings. After that, I would pay everyone else.

In my view, the very last part, "and prosper" was the most important. It meant I would prosper if I invested the money I saved. In effect, over time, it would let my saved money start making money as well. Right then, I remembered hearing a friend's grandfather talk about his business. He had been poor growing up, having very little, but as a young man, he religiously saved money. Eventually, he got a loan to buy a piece of land that appreciated into considerable value. I realized this was exactly what the Clue Bird's advice was all about.

In other words, I was going to have to work hard to earn enough money to cover my living expenses. That's what a large group of people do. However, I wanted to be in that somewhat smaller group of hard workers who pay themselves first. The ones capable of dealing with unexpected expenses, like fixing a broken-down car.

My ultimate goal was to be in an even smaller group. This last group lets their saved money earn additional money by investing it and letting it work alongside the income from their jobs. I wanted to grow my money over time by acquiring stocks, bonds, real estate, operating a business, and so on—to prosper like my friend's grandfather did.

Back when I was growing up, my grandmother would sometimes pay us for doing various chores. I stashed my money in a little sack and hid it in a dresser drawer. That sack represented all my worldly treasures. Occasionally, when alone, I would take it out and hold the coins. Even though it was maybe just a quarter or a couple of dimes and nickels mixed with about a dozen pennies. It felt great to have real money in my hands.

By analyzing the Clue Bird's message, for the first time in my young life, I equated a coin with something else. I realized my dime, a little piece of silver, represented an entire day of swimming at the community pool—something we could do only once a year. It then occurred to me that the money we all worked for was really a medium of exchange.

Applying the message

After working for a while, a kid understands that getting a job to earn money is going to be a lifelong proposition. Accepting that we'll work for the rest of our lives is like putting a saddle on ourselves. Much like taming a young horse for the first time, a trainer doesn't know what to expect. That scared horse might spook or become belligerent to the point of being dangerous, but after repeatedly placing a saddle on its back, the horse finally calms down.

After working with the horse for days, trainers know when to try mounting it for the first time. Once again, it's anybody's guess how that will turn out. Sooner or later, the horse accepts all of it. It stubbornly adjusts to domestication, proving to be steady and dependable for years to come.

Like a horse tamer, when my kids were young, all I asked was that they do chores and help around the house. Having them grow up to be successful in school was my priority. With a little give and take, they settled into doing what I asked of them.

I was in high school when I strapped on my saddle. I started working as a dishwasher in a local restaurant, working only about twenty hours a week to stay ahead in school. It was my first employee/employer relationship. That meant, unlike at home where I could vocalize ad nauseam my gripes and complaints, at work that type of behavior wasn't tolerated.

My boss told me what to do and how much time I had to accomplish it, along with other tasks. Employees also had to follow a dress code. How things worked wasn't up to me; they told me to show up on time and leave when directed. No one ever sought out my excellent advice on how to better run the restaurant—nor did anyone care. There was no getting around it: I felt as though I had put a bridle in my mouth and a saddle on my back.

Observing the employees on that job gave me an unexpected new perspective about my life. I was surprised to find the workers were shockingly as old as my parents. Really old. That observation chilled me. I started thinking high school might be far more valuable to me than I had ever suspected. Years later, I discussed this change in perspective with my kids. I shared how I figured out how quitting high school to take a full-time job would have been selling myself short.

By quitting, I would never have attained any of my goals. Further, because of my part-time job, I decided staying in school to excel in that arena was best for me. Ironically, I didn't get this perspective from counselors, teachers, my parents, or classmates, but simply from having a job.

Many of my friends had jobs in all sorts of businesses such as in construction, landscaping, clerical, and so on. At school, we often discussed and compared our experiences. We came to the unanimous conclusion: it's called work because it was the hardest thing we had ever done. At the same time, our studies and activities in high school didn't feel like work anymore.

A part-time job might not only let kids earn money, but also serve as a catalyst for reshaping their attitudes about the importance of doing well in school. After working at a real job, feeling what it was like to be in the trenches, I started to feel the need for interpersonal exploration.

I remembered reading somewhere not deciding about something is really a decision to not decide. I finally started feeling the need to address my future career. I asked myself, "What do I want to do?" It was a tough question for me to answer.

However, I knew I needed to decide because it was more important to me than not deciding at all. I discussed saving money when my kids took their first jobs. I explained that their entire life would be dominated by their work, so why not make sure it was also dominated by their savings?

The saving principle

Kids need very few things, yet they are bombarded with ads or persuaded by classmates to buy things they supposedly need, when it's clearly just acquiring things they want. I bring this up because my discussions with my kids about saving a small part of their earnings focused on helping them lose their *spend it all* mentality.

As human beings, we're supposedly the smartest inhabitants on the planet. I told my kids to learn from nature by studying a squirrel. Squirrels are driven by instincts and shaped by thousands of years of genetic information passed down from a long line of the best squirrels. So, up and running, a little squirrel with no schooling, religiously lives by the law of minimal effort.

That means it does nothing that doesn't directly support its survival. It forages for food, finds a safe suitable place to rest, cares for its young and fights for its survival every day until it dies. But another thing this squirrel and a few other creatures of nature do is save for the future. For these habitual savers, storing food is a matter of life or death. They live by the law of minimal effort, surviving by never wasting energy or resources. So, those that *squirrel it away*, as the old saying goes, are savers.

We're discussing two things most people should do from adulthood into old age. That's work and save. Bringing home a paycheck should automatically mean cashing it and then never failing to put away a certain amount in savings.

If you want to give your kids a wake-up call on this subject, just take them to the local mall to do some people watching for about an hour. While watching intently as people walk by, randomly ask your kids one of the four following questions to give them an idea.

✓ Is that person a saver or a spender and why?
✓ Does that person take care of themselves to live a long and healthy life?
✓ Does that person have enough savings to dip into until they die with some money left over? Why?
✓ Since that person looks like they've worked for a long time, why do they appear to be broke?

I did this with my kids often to impress upon them the need to be savers for life. The ultimate question is: "Do you want your kids to become that old and broke person someday?" Of course not.

They will work for most of their lives, but will they be savers or spenders? If they become spenders for their entire lives, they'll live paycheck to paycheck.

They'll often find themselves in a pinch because they lack the funds to cover something that comes up unexpectedly, such as a car repair or medical bill. For most of their lives as spenders, they will certainly be behind on their bills. Their lives will be a financial struggle that never goes away.

We should teach kids to manage debt by only borrowing money for a business or a home. Emphasize that they should avoid all other debt, such as the consumer debt many people needlessly acquire by buying silly things such as a new car or boat.

It's fine for them to buy whatever they want, but if they need debt to do so, they aren't ready for those things just yet. They should simply wait until they can pay cash for these items to stay on the correct path in their journey to prosperity.

Remember, if they're borrowing money like my old friend Ted, they're spending way too much. They must adjust their spending and live below their means in order to always save first.

Lastly, as their savings pile up, they shouldn't spend that money on just anything. Saved money should be earmarked only for investing in an asset of their choosing, allowing their savings to make them more money. With their savings making money, they are prospering.

Finally, when their money makes more money than they do from working, your kids have attained financial freedom. They can take off their saddles. At this juncture, for the first time since childhood, they can do whatever they choose. From your teaching, they have acquired the gift of financial wisdom, which they can pass on to their children.

That's it. Your kids can become financially free, unbridled by debts, obligations, and endless lists of have-to-dos. They will have earned the free time to enrich the lives of as many people as they choose, while being free to do whatever they wish.

Work hard, always pay yourself first, & prosper.

1- Work hard. Save hard. Focus on your dreams when choosing a career. Pick your dreams and passionately pursue them like you own them until you finally experience them.

2- Pay yourself first, then your bills. If difficult, curb your spending, not your savings. Wild animals are natural savers, and you should be too.

3- Bringing home a paycheck should start a habit of cashing your paycheck and simultaneously adding a certain amount into your savings.

4- Invest your money saved over a period, letting it make money as well. Doing this makes becoming well-off and financially free doable for practically all of us.

5- When your saved money makes more money than you do working, you have obtained financial freedom. You may quit working.

Lesson 12

Victor Or Victim

WE SPEND YEARS watching our kids grow up. As newborns, getting through a day of life takes maximum effort. As toddlers, they don't want to sleep because they might miss something. They fight sleep until they nod off in a moment, like switching off a light. I found it exciting to experience being a dad.

My kids had boundless energy and a wholesome zest for life, but as they grew, I noticed the nonstop learning they endured began to feel like a struggle to them. Their first battle was learning to walk and talk, then more stuff got piled on like brushing teeth, riding a bike, and starting school.

With school came T-ball, soccer, gymnastics, and studies. It took many private moments to console and challenge them to keep trying. During their first year of little league, I noticed the good players—the stars. My kids were not in that small group. However, after a couple of years, they climbed the ladder into the ranks of best players, while many of the early stars became average players or were no longer on the team. I asked myself why.

I concluded it was about how these kids put up with the struggle. If it got to them, they found excuses and quit. They moved on, losing a chance to become exceptional at something. It was a choice.

The other kids kept showing up, never losing their kid-like enthusiasm, and often with less natural talent, became skillful players. With my kids, I remained vigilant about getting ahead of their desire to give up. I coached them to learn from their struggles and become victors for life. In time, they embraced struggles as a gift, not a problem.

Without a doubt, skill development is never a steady or predictable upward climb toward excellence. Learning is hard. Whenever my kids wanted to give up, we'd discuss their options by focusing on their progress. I would help them calm down, take a moment to think back to their early days, and then ask that they put themselves in the old mindset of learning a new skill. I'd have them think about how hard it was learning to play piano, baseball, golf, theater, or whatever they'd spent countless hours learning to do.

Their level of frustration over fractions was particularly high. "How could anything be that complicated?" they moaned, as I frantically cut up fruit and a pie to serve as examples. They usually just wanted to give up or go to bed.

High school baseball was yet another quantum leap for my kids as they struggled to master the game. It's when physical size and strength matter because vastly improved pitching makes batting even harder. With these changes, some longtime Little Leaguers drop by the wayside. They quit playing because high school tryouts forced them to measure up, and they got cut because they lacked skill development.

There were also students who faced challenges in the classroom, which meant they failed to meet the grade requirements to play sports. During the high school years, classmates, teammates, or club members may drop out of school or an extracurricular activity for a valid reason like bad grades, illness, or becoming ineligible. Sometimes, they mysteriously quit for no apparent reason. No one knows why—they just quit.

I recall my baseball activities back when I was in high school, when they had just invented television. I was beaten out at second base by a freshman. It was only because I missed a couple of practices, I repeatedly told myself, desperately trying to find an excuse. However, I was just going along, doing the minimum I could get by with. I was coasting. Anyway, out of my frustration with myself, I got in a fight at practice.

Afterward, I decided to quit the team the next day. I was in a total state of misery, wanting to quit everything. That night, a strange feeling came over me in a dream. A little bird was sitting on my shoulder. Out of nowhere, he said, "Ultimately, every choice you make under duress will determine whether you are a victor or a victim."

I jumped up in my pitch-black room and turned on the lights to look at myself in the mirror. The words rang true to me. I can still remember that moment in full color. What the little bird said was the absolute truth about my life up to that point.

Back then, I was cashing in and quitting on myself. I was choosing to be a victim by sacrificing my dreams. I was tired of the constant struggle, putting less and less effort into every aspect of my life.

My room was a mess, and I was way behind in my schoolwork. Yes, looking back, I was choosing to become a victim. With the Clue Bird's advice, I clearly saw all my issues were self-imposed. I was the one causing my own frustrations with my nonstop, immature self-talk and always blaming others, thinking life is not fair, or saying it's just too hard and on and on.

Deciphering the message

I looked at everything in my life that night. My room had been appropriately described by family as a pigsty. I was embarrassed. Thinking no one should live like this, I felt disgusted and cleaned my room that night. The next morning, I took out several bags of trash. It was clear that choosing to quit baseball and even high school would be quitting on me.

Plain and simple, it would have been giving up on things and taking the easy way out by not doing what I was fully capable of doing with the correct attitude. It also dawned on me that quitting would probably become my new lifelong habit. I thought, "If I quit then what's next?"

Looking down the road, all I could see was how I might end up quitting a future job, a relationship, my kids someday, and on and on. If I did, quitting would become a habit and ruin my life as well as run my life. First, I wondered if being either a victor or a victim was simply about the choices we make reacting to the struggles of life.

It's not like some of us are born destined to be victims and others destined to be victors. It doesn't have anything to do with being smart, attractive, athletic, or being blessed at birth with unique gifts such as singing, musical talent, or having the smarts of an Albert Einstein. It boils down to a choice. I figured choosing to run my life by making decisions that ultimately defined me as either a victim or a victor was the key factor.

My predicament put me just one day away from making poor and irrational decisions. Those decisions would have made me a victim, setting in a victim mentality and living a life that would prove to be far below my talents and abilities. Luckily, I realized the duress I experienced in my life was often caused by me in the first place. By owning that, I could very clearly see the issues I faced. It meant I could change my life for the better.

So, I wondered if life was about a series of choices we make. If so, how do we first come to realize it? Further, how do we make the correct choices to become victors? I understood that first I had to accept that living and growing up is a constant struggle. I saw how everything— learning to walk, tying your shoes, schoolwork, and becoming excellent at practically anything in life—is a struggle at first.

Unfortunately, somewhere along the path of growing up, I got tired of the seemingly endless journey. I almost decided to quit something, to give up in a desire to seek a path of less struggle and difficulty. This would have been my first decision to become a victim. It would have meant sacrificing or selling myself for less than I was worth.

Focusing on the part of the message that said, "Ultimately, every choice you make under duress will determine whether you are a victor or a victim," gave me insight. Even being agitated and under duress, I had to make a life-changing choice. Up to that point, I thought the pressures, disappointments, and failures I experienced put me in a position of having to just put up with all of it. I felt stuck. However, after the Clue Bird's visit, I knew it was up to me to decide whether to be a victim or a victor.

My situation was my own problem. My grades were poor, and it was not because I couldn't do the work. I was lazy. I decided to apply myself with focused effort in each class on my schedule. Once again, as to baseball, in a moment of real honesty, I admitted it was my fault that I lost my starting position. Remembering how much I loved baseball restored my *desire to play*. It felt good to feel that way once again.

Before the message, I was close to choosing to become a victim for life. Instead, I adamantly chose to become a victor and went on seeking to be extraordinary in many things. I taught my kids this lesson, and they are victors for life too.

Applying the message

All kids vie to become good at something. They fight, struggle, and press on in their attempts to excel, and somewhere on that line of progression, they sometimes run out of fight. They simply quit. A friend of mine, who is a retired professional football player, told me he met people from all over during his playing days. Invariably, they would sooner or later, bring up stories about their old football days back in high school.

Shaking his head, he said it would always go something like, "Yeah, I played football back in the day and I was pretty good. I even had a few offers to play ball in college, but I_____." He said it was time for them to fill in the blank to finish their stories. What they'd say was their stand-in excuse for why they had quit the sport. It would be something like they blew out a knee, had to join the military, had to get a job to support the family, and on and on.

He stated they both knew it was a well-rehearsed lie they had been using for a long time. He continued, saying it was a *victor-or-victim moment* in their lives. My friend added that from where he stood, after all these years, he realized it's fine to play high school football and, after your senior season, with tears in your eyes and a chest full of pride, to proudly hang up your cleats for good. If you played, you still get to hang on to your well-earned letterman's jacket.

According to him, it's also fine to play in college and then hang up your cleats. As for professional players, he said, "We all know when it's our time to call it quits." There's a natural way to progress through your chosen path in life, whether it's football, music, theater, or other sports. They all require passion, hard work, and effort to become extraordinary at them.

The real issue is when people simply quit. What honor is there in quitting? Sometimes, quitting is your victor-or-victim moment. Let's explore victor or a victim by looking up the precise definition of those words to avoid misunderstanding. According to my leather-bound, handwritten Civil War version of Webster's dictionary, a victor is *a winner in a battle or a struggle.* A victim is *someone or something killed, destroyed, sacrificed, and more—one who suffers some loss.*

I think *victor* pertains to a winner in a struggle. Whether it's learning to tie your shoes as a toddler or grasping high school chemistry, life is filled with struggle. Everyone has to embrace it. The irony is that although children grow physically and mentally for almost twenty years, they're not yet fully prepared to conquer the world. It gets harder and harder.

The definition of victim is someone who was killed, destroyed, sacrificed, and more. To expand on the definition, let's look at sacrificed. It means giving up one thing for the sake of another or to sell at less than the supposed value.

To summarize, a victim is someone who is sacrificed. That means they gave up one thing for the sake of another or sold something at less than its supposed value. With that in mind, let's reflect on kids who quit something—such as school, a sport, or any extracurricular activity. I think it becomes noticeably clear they became victims by choice. They sacrificed one thing for another. They sold themselves out at far less than their value.

Sometimes life can feel like shadow boxing. It's us, in a room, against a lamp without a lampshade. No matter how much we grow, our shadow opponent grows too, making our struggle feel continuous and unrelenting. That's why I taught my kids not to look at their struggles as a problem, but just a manageable part of life, much like breathing, eating, and sleeping. Doing that ends those overwhelming feelings and the fear of dire consequences.

Everyone has to deal with daily struggles. Learning to label issues in a new way makes our lives much easier. With my kids, nothing physically changed, but they might have gotten the *kid in them* back, which they had somehow lost along the way in life.

Victors own it

Let's decide if what the Clue Bird told me is still true today. First, I think our lives are full of choices like where to park, whether to go to a movie, what to eat, and on and on. We're bombarded with choices every day. Yet the Clue Bird's message is about the big choices we make under duress. In high school, I was under duress, and it almost caused me to quit baseball—maybe even high school itself. To this day, I'm grateful I didn't.

My kids had to learn to do many things, but they only wanted to do things that made them feel happy. That's living with the *kid in you*. Many high school students, by mislabeling struggles as problems, slowly kill off that kid. It's important to find ways to keep the kid inside alive—never let your kids kill off the kid in them. I vowed that on my deathbed I would still be a kid at heart. I challenged my kids to live their lives in the same manner.

Experiencing setbacks, sometimes kids, in a private moment, think they're the only ones who have certain issues. This thinking only adds to their frustration. Well, the good news is, they're not alone. I often advised my kids to just ask a classmate how they felt. Every time, they quickly discovered many of their classmates felt the same way. This helped them accept that life is a constant struggle. I found the best way to get my kids to deal with learning difficult things was to help them embrace the struggle by smiling and asking the world, "Is that all you got?"

Redefine the word struggle with your children to help them look at their world with a little bit of the kid in them. Teach them that what they are currently calling a struggle, is just an opportunity. Ask them to accept the struggle to get excellent grades in school. Help them start looking at schoolwork as an opportunity. For sure, it requires a lot of effort, but it's not like struggling to dig a ditch in the scorching sun with a hand shovel or storm a beach in a war zone.

Struggling is tiresome, making us want to quit. Yet doing the same tasks while thinking of them as practice and personal development implies a payoff for the effort. It makes us feel good about ourselves. So, after all of this, it boils down to being either a victor or a victim. The question for every kid is: What's it going to be? Ten years from now, how will your kids answer this question about themselves? How will people who know them describe them?

Being a victor or a victim is about choice. If a kid decides to do something and then becomes frustrated if it gets too hard, they're faced with the choice to become a victor or a victim. Commitment to seeing things through, no matter what, makes you a victor. I once overheard a conversation between a young lieutenant who was going off to pilot training and his visiting friends. They were telling him he wouldn't make it because he didn't have what it took. "It's too hard for you," they said. He told them he would leave pilot training either with wings on his chest or dead. How do you think he did? Be a victor.

Victors have the right attitude. When an issue needs to be eliminated or vanquished, they first own it. They take it on as their issue. Next, they list ways to fix it. They pick the best course of action and execute it until the issue is gone from their lives. Then they ask the world, with a smile, "Is that all you got?" and move on.

Yes, the Clue Bird's message is still relevant. It can help your kids keep their kid-like attitudes and find a way to rise to the top. It will help them feel as if they can't wait to do something new or try something hard. *I can do it, and I am a winner*, are feelings we were all born with.

These are precious feelings to keep alive, no matter if you're young or old. We need to keep that feeling alive in kids by challenging them to do even more—to become the victors they were born to be. Embrace the struggle.

Every choice made under duress deter-mines whether you are a victor or a victim.

1- Don't let the struggle get to you. Learning practically everything is a constant struggle. Struggles may feel like a constant force of nature.

2- Embrace your struggles by always smiling, while asking the world, "Is that all you got?" Learn from struggles and become a victor for life, embracing each struggle as a gift, not a problem.

3- Learning varies with age, but struggles remain the same. Deal with your struggles by embracing them as gifts that highlight your shortcomings, showing you where to improve.

4- Quitting will probably become a life-long habit. Quitting as a habit, will both ruin your life as well as run your life.

5- Viewing life as a struggle will tire you, making you want to quit. Focus on your payoff and not the struggle, always viewing your struggle as an opportunity, not the problem.

LESSON 13

BE GRATEFUL

As TODDLERS, MY kids were all about being. I would watch them for hours as they played. They could make a toy out of anything. Sometimes, they played with our dog or explored room after room in our house. No matter what, they were happy. With the passage of time, however, life got in the way and started them down the road of doing things—simple things at first, like getting dressed. Later, we had them brush their own teeth and help around the house.

School was the next troubling thing they had to do, along with all the sports, social activities, and schoolwork. In time, my kids went from being... to doing. They became doers. In the rush to get kids to do things, mixed with constant pressure to do even more and harder things, many kids stop being.

When I spoke with my kids about injecting gratitude into their lives, they asked in unison, "What's in it for me?" They wanted to know the payoff for doing one more thing in their already busy lives. Gratitude, I told them, wasn't something they had to study, write a theme about, memorize, recite, or learn to sing. It's simply being thankful, as often as possible, every day. That's not too hard.

I know, because my experience with gratitude came early, from my paternal grandmother who raised me. Her whole family was poor, making it impossible for anyone to attend school for more than a few years. She herself only went as far as the third grade. Unfortunately, when she was growing up, kids left school as soon as they could to help support their families, and still, we didn't have much. We lived in a rural community where we eked out our existence with little communal help.

Religiously, my grandmother would drag me to church on Wednesday nights, Saturdays, and Sundays without fail. At the entrance, there was a large table where my grandmother would place what she had brought to share with those who had even less. She brought practically anything to give away—even when it was something we could have used. I found it a little annoying.

Out of frustration, I got up the courage to ask her why she took from us to give to others. She calmly told me we were very blessed and had more than we needed. Out of gratitude, she felt compelled to share our blessings with others in need. That shut me up. Summing things up, my grandma suggested I spend time each day thinking of things to feel grateful for. She said it would make me feel wealthy and generous.

That night, while sound asleep, that beautiful little clue bird landed on my shoulder to whisper, "At your core, be grateful, happy, and joyful while you're busy at doing." Feeling excited, I went to my desk and carefully wrote down what I had heard, knowing I'd probably spend the rest of the night trying to understand what it meant.

Deciphering the message

I broke down what he said into pieces to analyze it. "At your core" was a mystery for a minute, but I decided that *core* meant... me—a human being. Not the flesh-and-bones part but the essence part. The spiritual part. The part I had been ignoring for years being so busy doing things while growing up. The imagination part and most important, the feelings part of me.

I saw how I had turned myself into a little robot, madly running around just doing things. I never stopped to *just be* me for a while, to be thankful for my grandmother or to feel happy about my family.

The next part of the Clue Bird's message was, "Be grateful, happy and joyful." I admitted I had never been joyful. I was too busy doing stuff, trying not to fall behind. Sitting there with just my thoughts, I realized I couldn't *do* grateful, happy, or joyful. I could only *be* them. As a test, for a few moments, I tried to be grateful. Surprisingly, those few moments were enough.

Continuing, I spent some time just feeling happy. It was easy, because I realized so many unnoticed things in my life brought me happiness—my grandma, family, good health, school, friends, sports and on and on came to mind. I became overwhelmed with a sudden happiness that first made me smile broadly, then burst into tears. Feeling grateful was like running into an old friend I had ignored while being too busy to notice them.

Curiously, it was the little things that came to mind. It wasn't going to a theme park, on vacation, or to the beach. It was things like my dog, my brother, watching a movie with my family, getting ice cream. I sat there alone, feeling overwhelmed—being happy.

It was a feeling I'd been without for a long time, while crazily doing the many things required of me. I felt blessed and wealthy for the first time ever. Yet nothing in my life had changed. I reasoned that if we were abundant enough to give things away to others, then we had nothing to worry about. A weight seemed to have been taken off my shoulders.

Next, I spent time being joyful. I felt that being joyful was a personal treasure. It was like being grateful and happy at the same time. It's a wholesome feeling of knowing everything is as it should be. I sat at my desk, understanding this was what I had been lacking. It filled the void in me. My heart swelled.

In an instant, I knew I needed to wash myself in gratefulness, allowing myself to feel happy and joyful every day. I knew this would ground me and be my anchor, no matter what life presented.

The last part of the Clue Bird's message was, "While you're busy at doing." This all made perfect sense to me. It was okay for me to be busy—no matter how old, everyone is probably busy doing things. But doing things couldn't be all I did. There had to be a balance between being and doing. That's what would make me whole. Complete me. I couldn't stop doing things or I wouldn't survive. Yet I figured I couldn't become so busy doing life that I never took time to just be.

Applying the message

Here are examples of tiny things any kid can be grateful for: running late they luckily caught a bus, a doctor's appointment of grave concern ended happily, or having a delicious lunch with their friends. It's easy. Through laughter, friendships, and on and on they can discover while going forward each day, how blessed they are. When this happens, kids start living a life filled with gratitude about everything. It's kind of how I felt escaping the coyotes that chased me the other night.

Another way to help kids practice gratitude is to ask them to take a moment to think of something they are thankful for. Have them notice how sweet it feels inside when they concentrate on their thankfulness. Doing this will help them discover that gratitude is not like taking a math class, but something that just is. It's free and wonderful.

Being grateful is more like learning to ride a bike. Initially, it's hard, and the rider is a little stiff and clumsy, but with practice, the rider becomes an ace. It happens quickly—in less than a day. Gratitude is the same way. With practice, we can maintain the balance between being and doing.

First, a kid begins to feel grateful for small things such as observing a beautiful butterfly, a sunset, or passing to the next grade at the end of a tough school year. As gratitude solidifies, they can expect offshoots such as becoming happy and overwhelmed with a strange yet delicious feeling of becoming joyful. This change in their core will ground them. These feelings will always be there when weathering the storms. Additionally, they will, without effort, experience random moments of generosity, kindness, and sharing.

Years ago, while visiting my son at a military hospital, someone knocked on his door. When I opened it, Sgt. Miller held out his hand. As we shook hands, I noticed he was missing a leg above the knee and his left arm. Smiling and guiding his wheelchair forward, he said he wanted to meet the patient living in *his room*. The same room he had occupied for several years while getting treatment for his combat injuries.

Sgt. Miller and my son talked nonstop about the war, combat, injuries, and life in general. After a long visit, Sgt. Miller finally bid us farewell. I decided to walk along with him to make sure he had adequate transportation for his ride home. At the elevator, he told me he felt like the luckiest man in the world because he got to come home to his wife and kids. He said, he was grateful.

Thankfully, the elevator doors closed quickly, so he didn't see my tears. I stood there thinking: if Sgt. Miller felt full of gratitude, as if he were the luckiest man in the world, then I didn't have the right to ever feel sorry for myself. I promised myself never to feel poor, unhappy, or to lack joy in my heart. To this day, whenever I teeter over, feeling like my old whiny self, I just remember Sgt. Miller. Instantly, I'd snap back to living my life as a victor, filled with gratitude.

First, be grateful

Developing kids at their core has nothing to do with math, science, and the like. It's about teaching gratitude. When kids hold gratitude in their hearts, they have a sense of completeness. Such kids are more likely to share, help others, and give generously. Gratitude and thankfulness are the doors to joy—plain and simple.

According to my handy handwritten dictionary, the one I carried during the Civil War—joy is *a very glad feeling, happiness, and delight.* Look around at the people you know. Do any of them walk around full of joy but aren't also grateful?

Gratitude makes joy possible. It's a great gift that changes kids back into human beings and not human doers. Help your kids reclaim the crucial balance between doing and being. Being grateful allows kids to be the gift in the room. With their display of generosity, kindness, and sharing, those around them will secretly emulate them. All of this lifts the lives of those around them. The payoff is huge. Their investment is minimal. Teach your kids to be grateful.

Remember, remind your kids it costs them nothing to feel gratitude. Start with the small stuff. Have them think about how blessed they are for their good health. How about having gratitude for their pet, siblings, parents, and families, or just a beautiful day? These are all blessings.

When children start looking at their lives in this way, feeling grateful will become automatic. They will learn to be grateful and busy at the same time. Without effort, they'll begin feeling blessed and thankful every day, everywhere they go.

Being grateful balances out our lives and possibly evens some spokes on our wheels of life. We must properly focus on all our spokes to ensure we have a balanced life. That means growing evenly and preventing ourselves from getting out of round, making life harder to navigate. The lesson here is to help kids be well-rounded by spreading our attention across all aspects of their development. The end result is a balanced life. It works.

Lastly, when my grandmother shared what little we had, I remember the look of gratitude in the eyes of the parishioners who picked up those things. Gratitude is a two-way experience where both the giver and the receiver win.

Fortunately, kids can expect to feel the gift of sharing, as it's connected to being grateful. In discussions with my kids, I insisted they fill in all the qualities that make up their beings while focusing on doing the things necessary to grow up and provide for themselves—and later their future families. Today, my kids realize adding gratitude to their beings was easy and effortless. They just needed to decide to become aware of the need to be grateful. In the blink of an eye, they became grateful.

You can feel joy while watching a beautiful sunset, so magnificent you simply pause from your busy day to just stand there in awe. In such quiet moments, a feeling of gratitude fills your spirit. Have you ever noticed that sometimes you also become overwhelmed with a feeling of being happy to the core?

Has a feeling of joyfulness ever washed over you in an odd moment? Personally, yes, I've experienced moments like this. They cast me into some kind of spell. I feel like I'm standing all alone, wrapped in contentment, feeling that it's just me and this beautiful sunset. During such times, I instantly feel gratitude, happiness, and joy all at once. It's so profound. Without thinking, the words *thank you* repeatedly spill out of my mouth.

My challenge to dads is to teach their kids about gratitude early—not later. It will prove to be a blessing to the entire family. It's a way of being down to the core. It's a gift that will change their lives while they go on doing whatever they are busy doing.

Remind your child that it takes little time or effort to be gracious. It's free. Teaching them this effortless, constant state of mind allows them to live a life they can enjoy and pass along to others. Teach them to be while they are busy doing.

At first, gratitude comes and goes, but eventually it will become a nonstop way of being—much like a heartbeat. They will know when it is not present. Maybe they'll need to remember someone like Sgt. Miller from time to time, just to keep themselves on track. Most of all, let's remember the Clue Bird said, "At your core, be grateful, happy, and joyful while you're busy at doing."

At your core, be grateful, happy, and joyful while you're busy doing.

1- Find a balance between doing and being. Rediscover who you are as a being, while you are busy doing.

2- Gratitude is the feeling of being thankful. Being grateful, as often as possible, balances out life and possibly evens some spokes on your wheel of life.

3- Add gratitude to your core, adding happiness, joy, generosity, kindness, and sharing to your core values. This will define you and your reactions to life, no matter the circumstances.

4- The attributes of gratitude can automatically become an active part of you again. They have always been in you lying dormant to your preoccupation with doing.

5- With gratitude, you become thankful for all your blessings. Gratitude is a two-way experience for both the giver and the receiver where everyone wins.

FIND YOUR CLUE BIRD

WE STARTED THIS journey together with a discussion about how the Clue Bird magically appears to whisper sage-like advice to help with life decisions. I believe this mysterious little bird is our subconscious mind, which knows all. It provides us with super accurate advice, especially in times of intense trouble. Many people claim they've never had a conscious Clue Bird experience. Maybe they just don't recognize it yet.

In times of duress, everything around us might be physically loud, confusing, and terrifying. In those moments, perhaps we can't consciously hear the Clue Bird. Still, we somehow press forward automatically, following our *sudden hunches*, leading us to make brilliant choices—sometimes saving lives. This is especially true for professions dealing in life-and-death situations. They regularly experience an out-of-nowhere sense of brilliance at the perfect moment. I take that as proof of the Clue Bird's existence.

Finding your Clue Bird isn't difficult, but looking at ourselves honestly makes us feel vulnerable. That's often where the Clue Bird finds us. I felt vulnerable when revealing how I dealt with my difficult moments growing up. Much of it was painful to remember. Possibly some of you also feel embarrassed about how you acted in high school or while in college. Using the Clue Bird's advice definitely helped me get through several of my tough issues.

As a single parent, I worked doubly hard to address my kids' struggles. Most of them dealt with the same issues I confronted growing up. Now, my adult children deal with those very issues with their own children. With the vast changes in our non-stop, fast-paced world, one expects the issues facing children to change from generation to generation—but they don't.

Each generation, from steam engines to jet airplanes, faced the same human issues, dilemmas and troubles as the one preceding them. Only our responses change. If I were speaking to my children today, maybe this is what I might say:

As my children, you are now confronting numerous issues growing up. Ironically, many of you are in the same place where we, your parents, were back when we were your age. Growing up, you are about to face the same issues we had to conquer. At birth, you were helpless as your caregivers, did one hundred percent of the lifting. Certainly, you don't remember all that. In your early years you started on your journey doing absolutely nothing for yourselves.

However, over the next twenty years you must begin to gradually, yet willingly, take on the responsibilities we once handled for you. You will probably resist taking on responsibilities at first. You will want to remain a child, but you must willingly transform into taking on your personal responsibilities.

The longer you fight and delay this transformation, the more pain and suffering you will experience growing up. This slow but steady transition allows you to successfully morph into a self-sufficient young adult. Mission accomplished.

We realize the most difficult part of raising children is making sure they're well balanced. To do this, we need to help them develop physically, mentally, and emotionally. It takes all three parts. We also know that when children fall behind in their mental and emotional growth, problems can arise. Problems such as failure in school and acting very immaturely.

Throughout this book, we saw how overcoming the conflict between physical, mental, and emotional growth is where all the hard work of growing up gets done. And you probably notice it gets harder around middle school age. The dilemma is knowing how soon to let them take on their own workload. The goal is to retire from being president of your child's *You, Inc.* You want to hand the job over to them.

If your child clings to irresponsibility, fighting, and struggling to not grow up, they will needlessly delay this transition. The personal cost to them will be exceedingly high. Therefore, get your child thinking like he's the president of his own *You, Inc.* as early as possible. That means before middle school starts. Delaying this transition may harm your child, preventing them from keeping up with the demands of growing up. They might even lose their job as president.

On the other hand, if you transition a child too early or too aggressively, they may suffer. Being too young for the overload of responsibility may result in costly mistakes. This will slow down the natural growth and progression from childhood to adulthood. When the transition is about right—you'll know it. Everyone concerned will feel good about the child's progress. In this scenario, most of his feedback is also positive. His grades are good, he has a great group of friends, and everything he does seems to fit nicely together. The success of this transition is without question up to your child.

Your children must willingly and eagerly take on the additional things asked of them by the adults in their lives. This requires giving up their innate desire to be without responsibilities. It means giving up their minimal-effort approach to living. It means they voluntarily shift to a hard work adult mindset.

We must steer our children to choose to be victors, not victims. Parents can learn a lesson from birds. When the day arrives, the parent bird encourages their darling little offspring to fly away, leaving the safety of the nest. The young ones fight, not wanting to go, but the parent knows letting the offspring stay will keep him from living his life to the fullest. Being a loving parent, it may nudge their young ones out of the nest. It's the same for us. Our young must fly away, causing both joy and sadness. Challenging children to become the best version of themselves they can become requires us to let go.

It is my sincere hope that the topics we addressed help you raise successful, well-balanced adults. As you do, refer to the discussions in this book. Use them as a starting point to ensure your child learns the lessons covered here. Show your children how to soar, blazing a trail through life in a way others will be in awe of, secretly admire, and wish to emulate.

Acknowledgements

There are so many people to thank for helping me with this book and turning it into a successful project, beginning with J, whose assistance and support made it all possible. I'm also deeply grateful to my Grandma, who loved me and shared her wisdom. She's proof that angels walk this earth. Though I never knew my dad, who died as a POW in the Korean War, I believe he would be proud of my brother and me.

Forever holding my heart are my wonderful kids and grandkids, who provided much of the material in this book.

Love you all so much.

About the Author

R. Wayne Browne is a successful businessman and former fighter pilot who doubled as a single parent—proof that bravery doesn't end when you step out of the cockpit or leave the boardroom. It just takes a different form in the living room, at the dining table, or while making lunches and drawing hearts on napkins.

Raising two kids on his own, he brings the same clarity, calmness, and mission-focused mindset to parenting that he once brought to high-stakes missions. But he'll be the first to tell you: no checklist or call sign could have prepared him for building a dad style from the ground up.

Blending real-life experience with thirteen life-lessons, he writes with honesty and deep respect for parents flying solo. His goal? To help moms and dads feel equipped, encouraged, and far from alone—no matter what the day (or the kids) throw their way.